NICKELODEON

SpongeBob SquarePants™

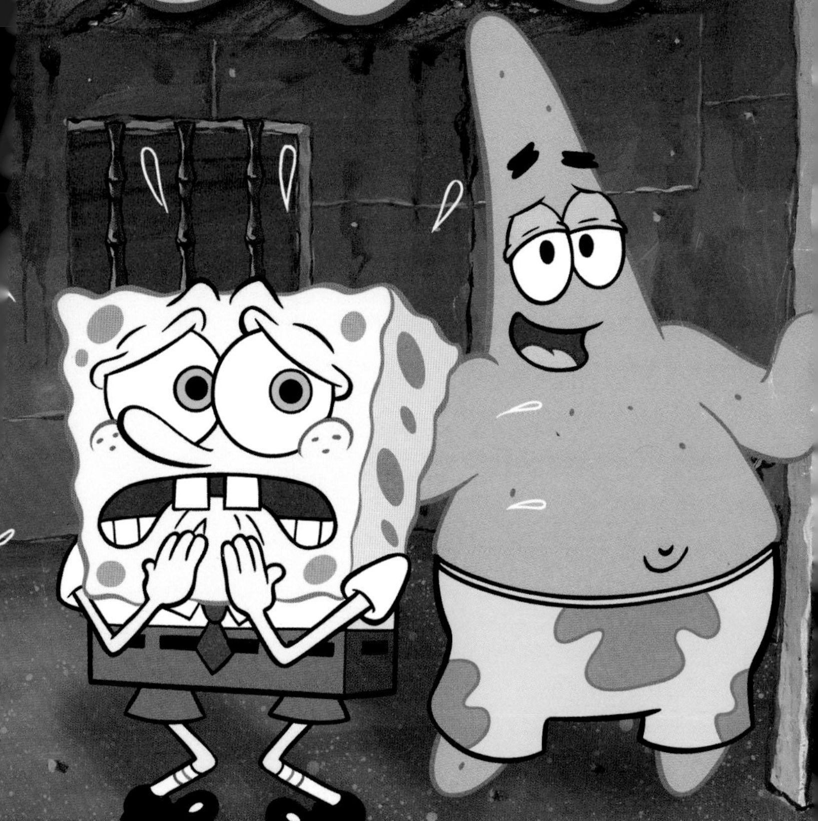

CRIME AND FUNISHMENT

Contributing Editor - Amy Court-Kaemon
Graphic Design and Lettering - Dave Snow
Graphic Artists - Tomás Montalvo-Lagos & Jennifer Nunn-Iwai
Cover Layout - Raymond Makowski

Editors - Elizabeth Hurchalla & Jod Kaftan
Digital Imaging Manager - Chris Buford
Pre-Press Manager - Antonio DePietro
Production Manager - Jennifer Miller
Art Director - Matt Alford
Managing Editor - Jill Freshney
Editorial Director - Jeremy Ross
VP of Production - Ron Klamert
President & C.O.O. - John Parker
Publisher & C.E.O. - Stuart Levy

Come visit us online at www.TOKYOPOP.com

A **TOKYOPOP** Cine-Manga® Book
TOKYOPOP Inc.
5900 Wilshire Blvd., Suite 2000, Los Angeles, CA 90036

SPONGEBOB SQUAREPANTS: CRIME AND FUNISHMENT

ISBN: 1-59182-576-8
First TOKYOPOP® printing: July 2004

10 9 8 7 6 5 4 3 2

Printed in U.S.A.

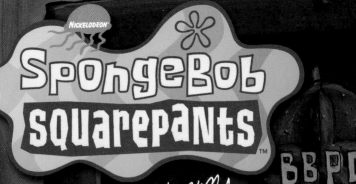

Nickelodeon

SpongeBob SquarePants™

Created by Stephen Hillenburg

CRIME AND FUNISHMENT

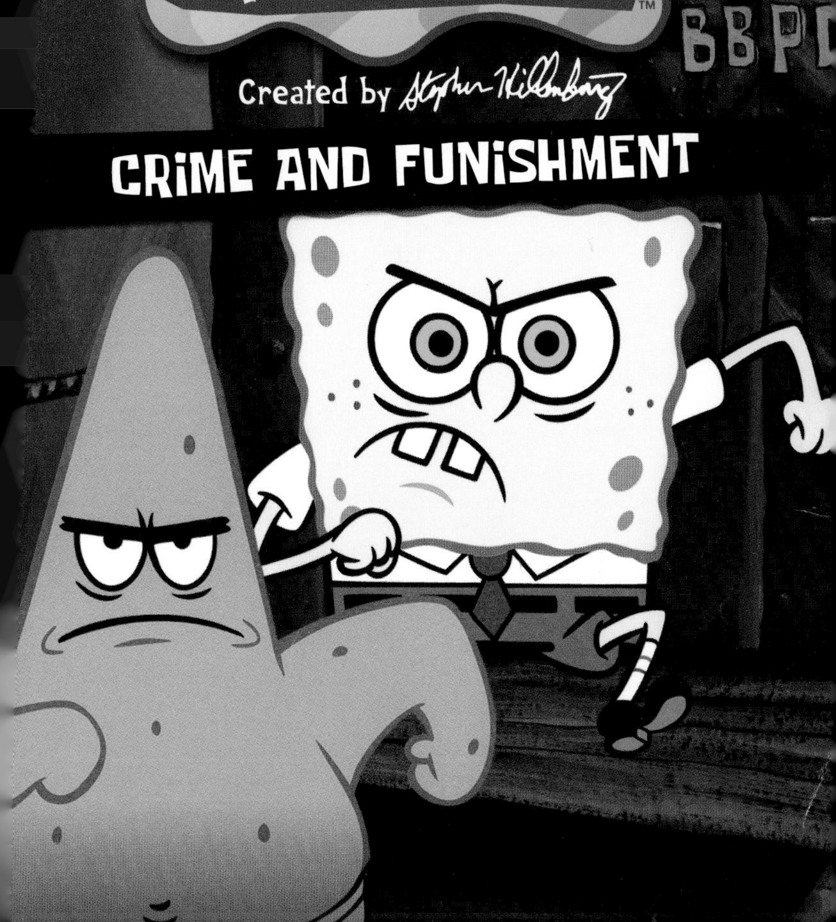
BBPD

TOKYOPOP®

LOS ANGELES · TOKYO · LONDON · HAMBURG

SpongeBob™
SQUAREPANTS

SPONGEBOB SQUAREPANTS An optimisti and friendly sea sponge who lives in a pineapple with his snail, Gary, and works as a fry cook at The Krusty Krab. He loves his job and is always looking on the bright side of everything.

SQUIDWARD TENTACLES: A squid who works as the cashier at The Krusty Krab. Unlike SpongeBob, Squidward tends to be negative about everything.

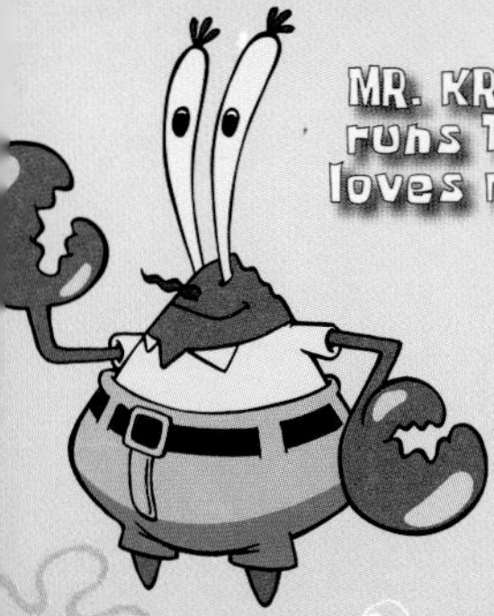

MR. KRABS: A crab who owns and runs The Krusty Krab. Mr. Krabs loves money and will do anything to avoid losing it.

MRS. PUFF: A pufferfish who runs a boating school.

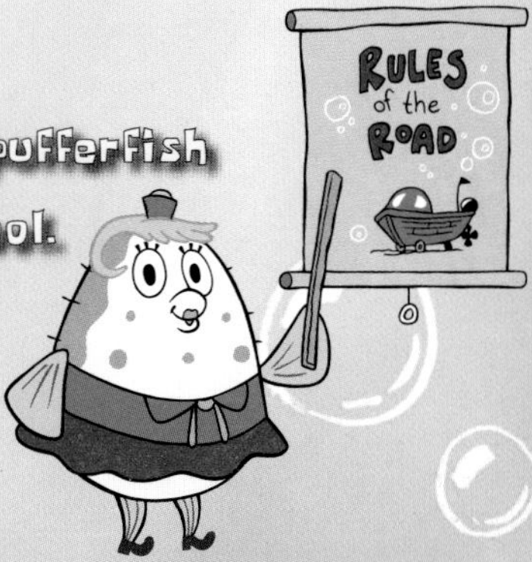
RULES of the ROAD

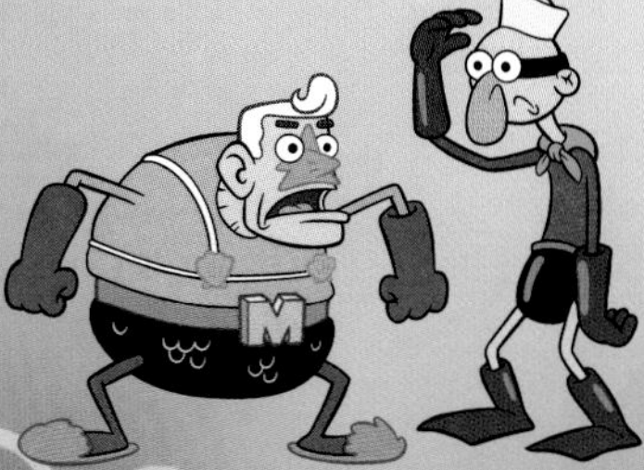

MERMAIDMAN AND BARNACLEBOY: Bikini Bottom's favorite superheroes.

SANDY: A thrill-seeking squirrel who loves extreme sports.

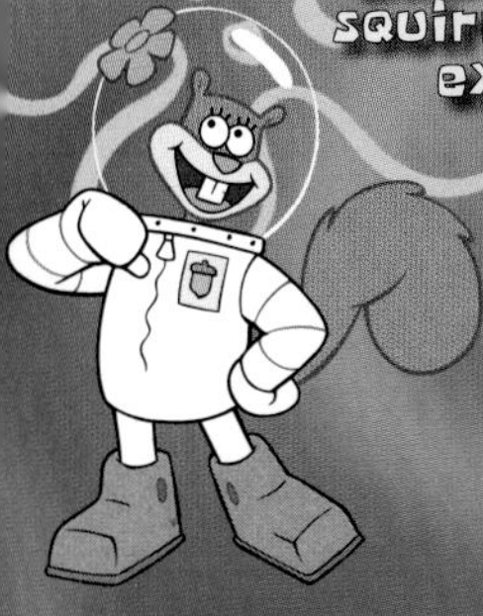

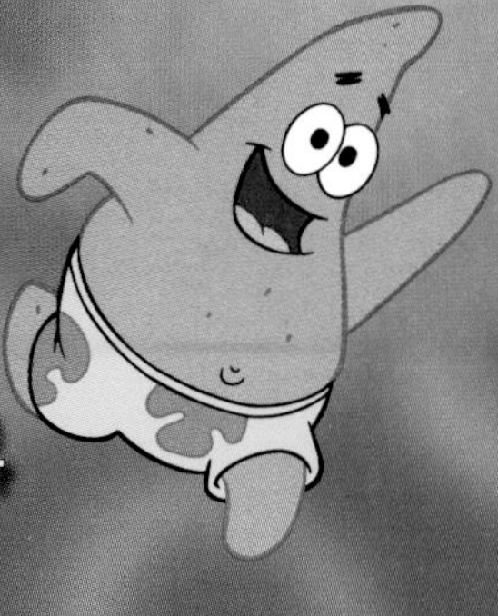

PATRICK STAR: A starfish who is SpongeBob's best friend and neighbor.

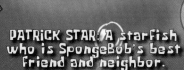

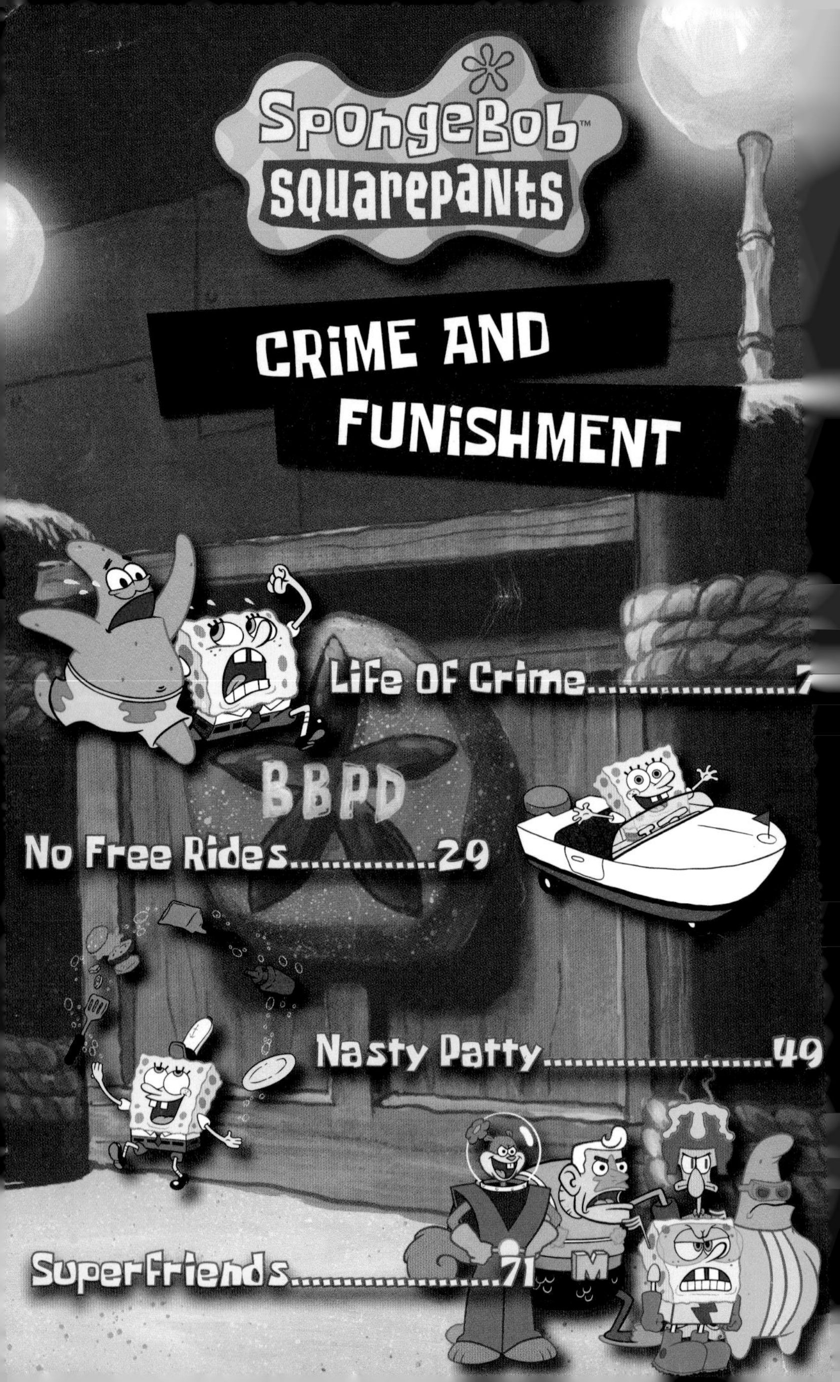
BBPD
M

SpongeBob SquarePants

CRIME AND FUNISHMENT

SpongeBob SquarePants

LIFE OF CRIME

by Jay Lender, William Reiss
and Mr. Lawrence

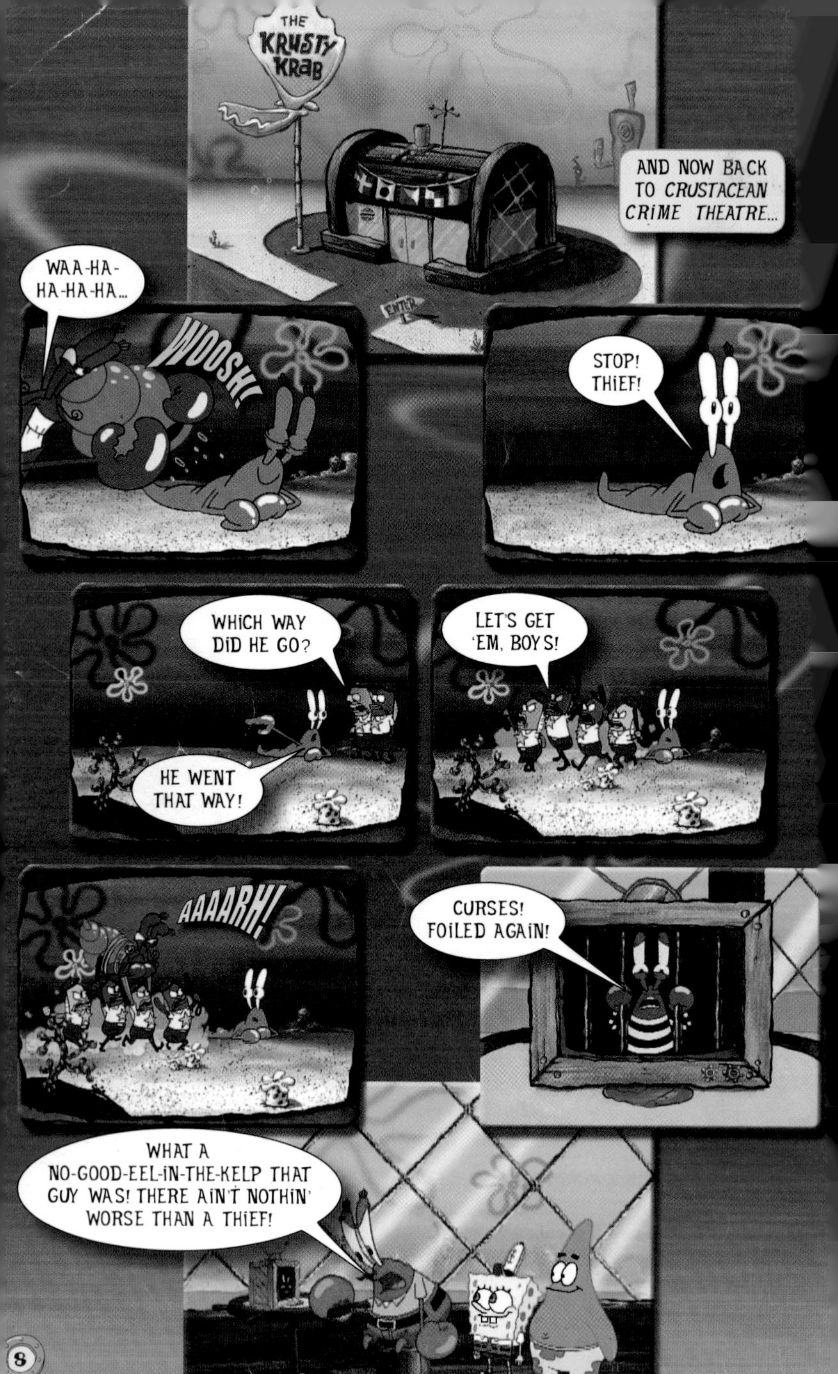
THE KRUSTY KRAB
AND NOW BACK TO CRUSTACEAN CRIME THEATRE...
WAA-HA-HA-HA-HA...
WOOSH!
STOP! THIEF!
WHICH WAY DID HE GO?
HE WENT THAT WAY!
LET'S GET 'EM, BOYS!
AAAARH!
CURSES! FOILED AGAIN!
WHAT A NO-GOOD-EEL-IN-THE-KELP THAT GUY WAS! THERE AIN'T NOTHIN' WORSE THAN A THIEF!

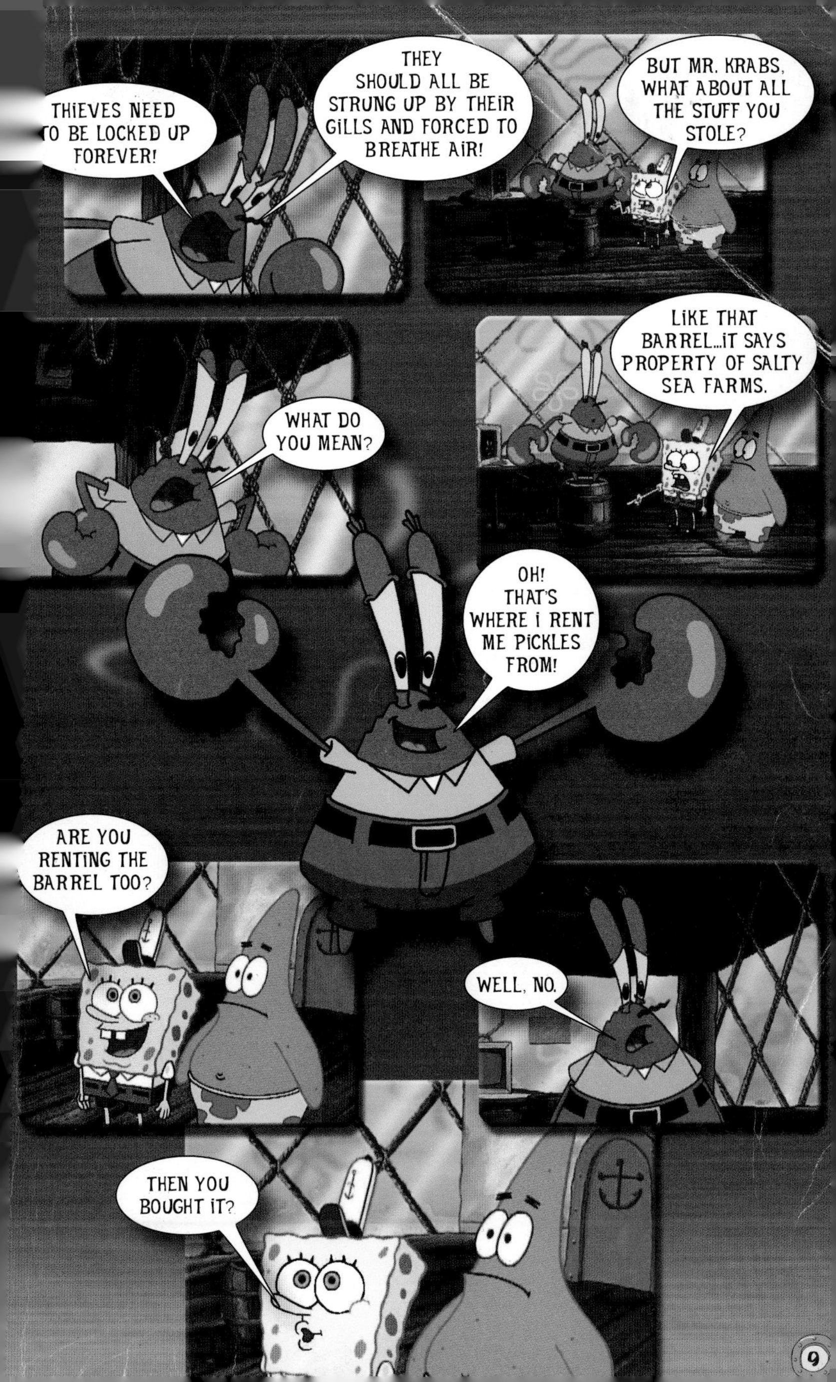
THIEVES NEED TO BE LOCKED UP FOREVER!
THEY SHOULD ALL BE STRUNG UP BY THEIR GILLS AND FORCED TO BREATHE AIR!
BUT MR. KRABS, WHAT ABOUT ALL THE STUFF YOU STOLE?
WHAT DO YOU MEAN?
LIKE THAT BARREL...IT SAYS PROPERTY OF SALTY SEA FARMS.
OH! THAT'S WHERE I RENT ME PICKLES FROM!
ARE YOU RENTING THE BARREL TOO?
WELL, NO.
THEN YOU BOUGHT IT?

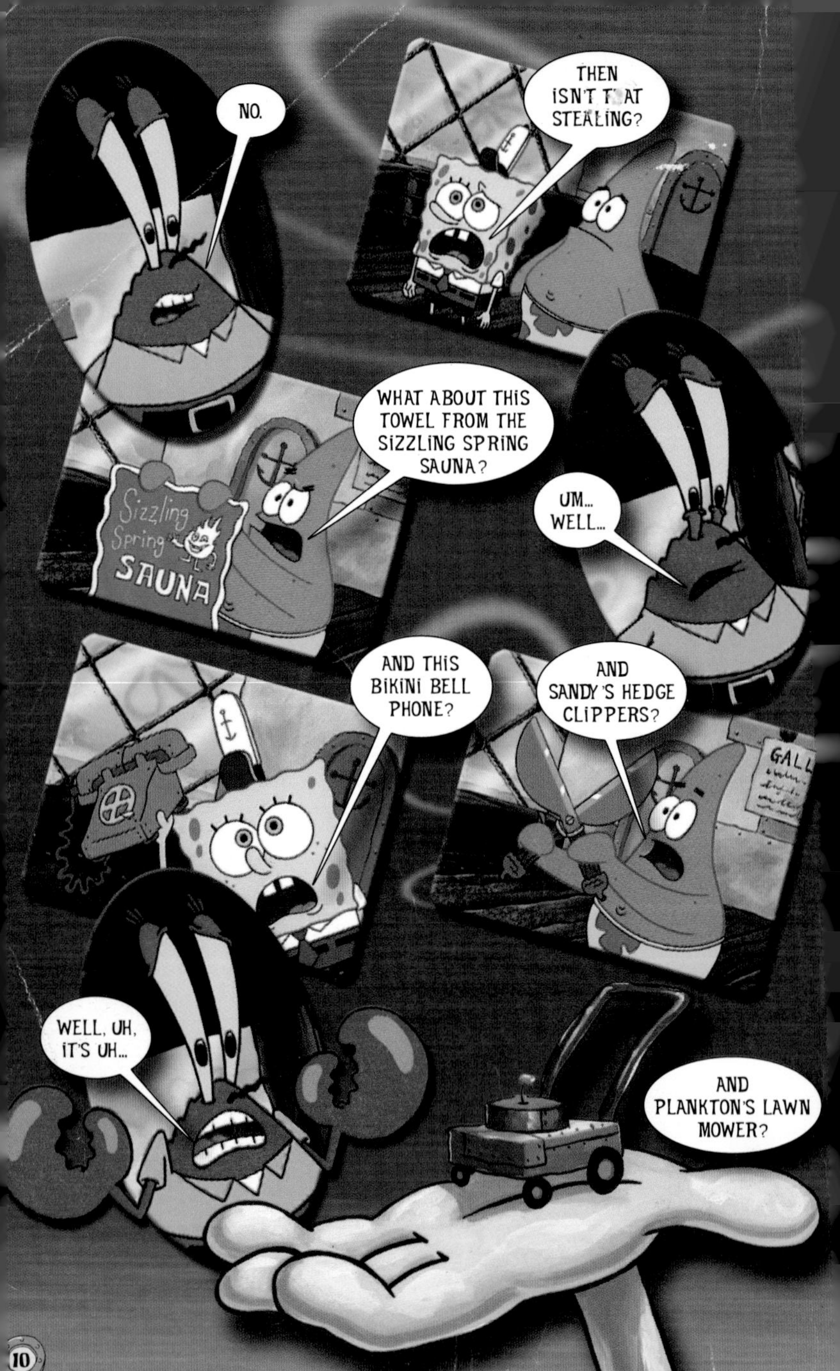
NO.
THEN ISN'T THAT STEALING?
WHAT ABOUT THIS TOWEL FROM THE SIZZLING SPRING SAUNA?
Sizzling Spring SAUNA
UM... WELL...
AND THIS BIKINI BELL PHONE?
AND SANDY'S HEDGE CLIPPERS?
WELL, UH, IT'S UH...
AND PLANKTON'S LAWN MOWER?

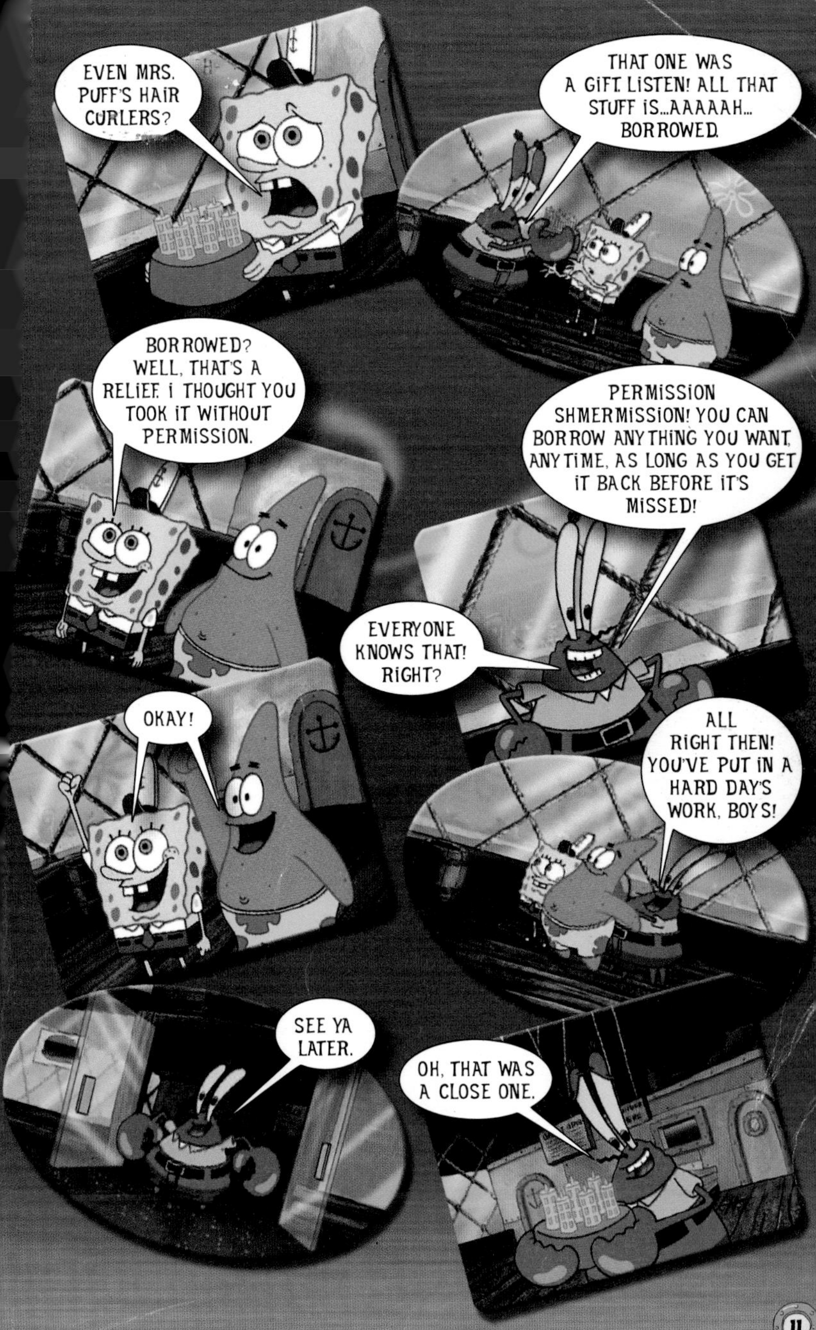

EVEN MRS. PUFF'S HAIR CURLERS?
THAT ONE WAS A GIFT. LISTEN! ALL THAT STUFF IS...AAAAAH... BORROWED.
BORROWED? WELL, THAT'S A RELIEF. I THOUGHT YOU TOOK IT WITHOUT PERMISSION.
PERMISSION SHMERMISSION! YOU CAN BORROW ANYTHING YOU WANT, ANYTIME, AS LONG AS YOU GET IT BACK BEFORE IT'S MISSED!
EVERYONE KNOWS THAT! RIGHT?
OKAY!
ALL RIGHT THEN! YOU'VE PUT IN A HARD DAY'S WORK, BOYS!
SEE YA LATER.
OH, THAT WAS A CLOSE ONE.

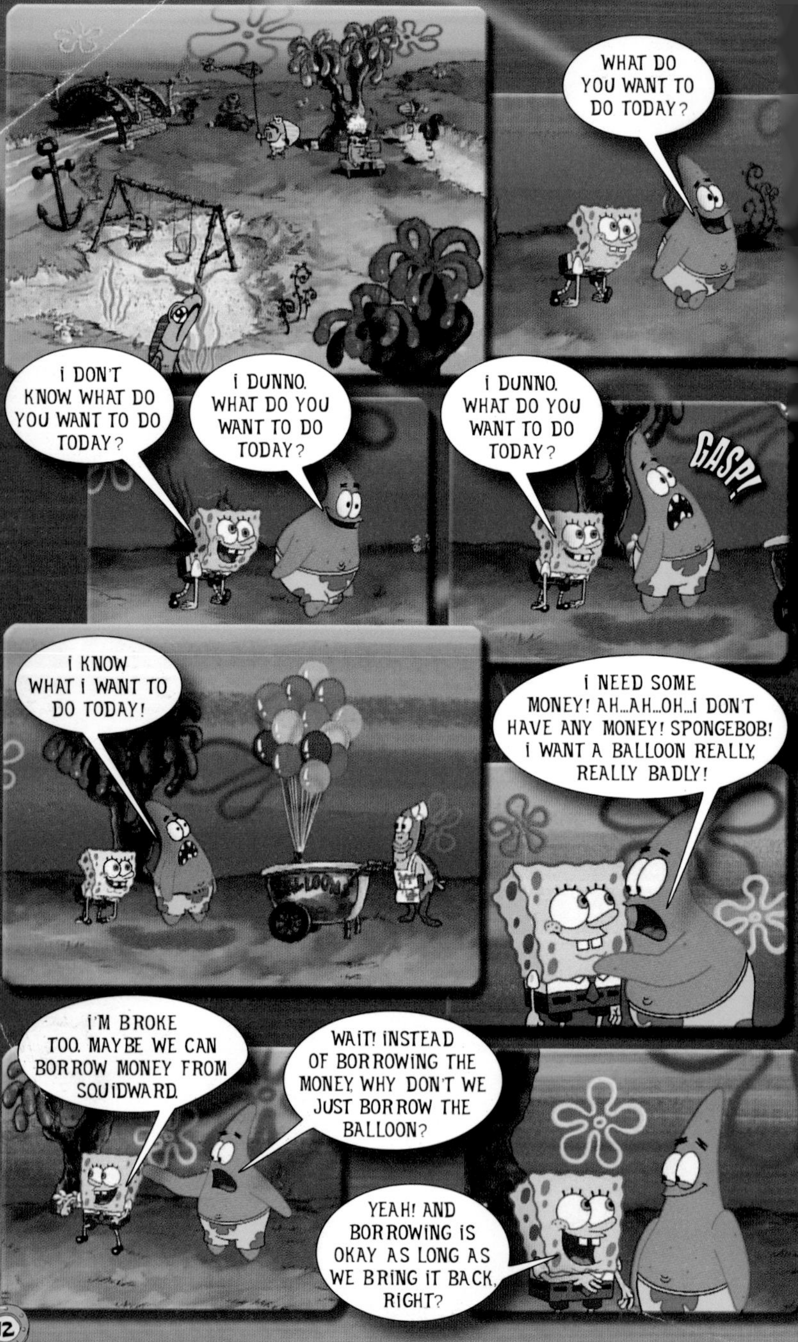
WHAT DO YOU WANT TO DO TODAY?
I DON'T KNOW. WHAT DO YOU WANT TO DO TODAY?
I DUNNO. WHAT DO YOU WANT TO DO TODAY?
I DUNNO. WHAT DO YOU WANT TO DO TODAY?
GASP!
I KNOW WHAT I WANT TO DO TODAY!
I NEED SOME MONEY! AH...AH...OH...I DON'T HAVE ANY MONEY! SPONGEBOB! I WANT A BALLOON REALLY, REALLY BADLY!
I'M BROKE TOO. MAYBE WE CAN BORROW MONEY FROM SQUIDWARD.
WAIT! INSTEAD OF BORROWING THE MONEY, WHY DON'T WE JUST BORROW THE BALLOON?
YEAH! AND BORROWING IS OKAY AS LONG AS WE BRING IT BACK, RIGHT?

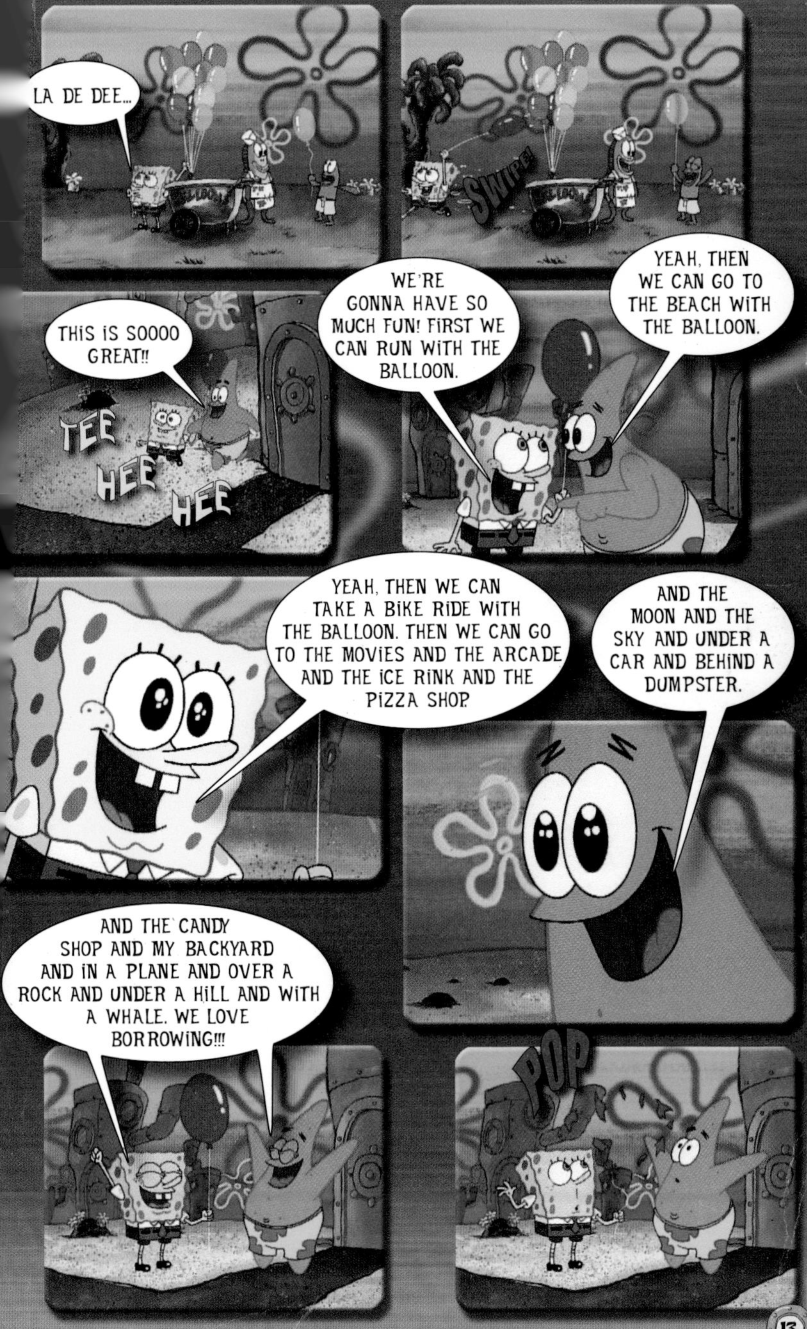

LA DE DEE...
SWIPE!
THIS IS SOOOO GREAT!!
TEE HEE HEE
WE'RE GONNA HAVE SO MUCH FUN! FIRST WE CAN RUN WITH THE BALLOON.
YEAH, THEN WE CAN GO TO THE BEACH WITH THE BALLOON.
YEAH, THEN WE CAN TAKE A BIKE RIDE WITH THE BALLOON. THEN WE CAN GO TO THE MOVIES AND THE ARCADE AND THE ICE RINK AND THE PIZZA SHOP.
AND THE MOON AND THE SKY AND UNDER A CAR AND BEHIND A DUMPSTER.
AND THE CANDY SHOP AND MY BACKYARD AND IN A PLANE AND OVER A ROCK AND UNDER A HILL AND WITH A WHALE. WE LOVE BORROWING!!!
POP

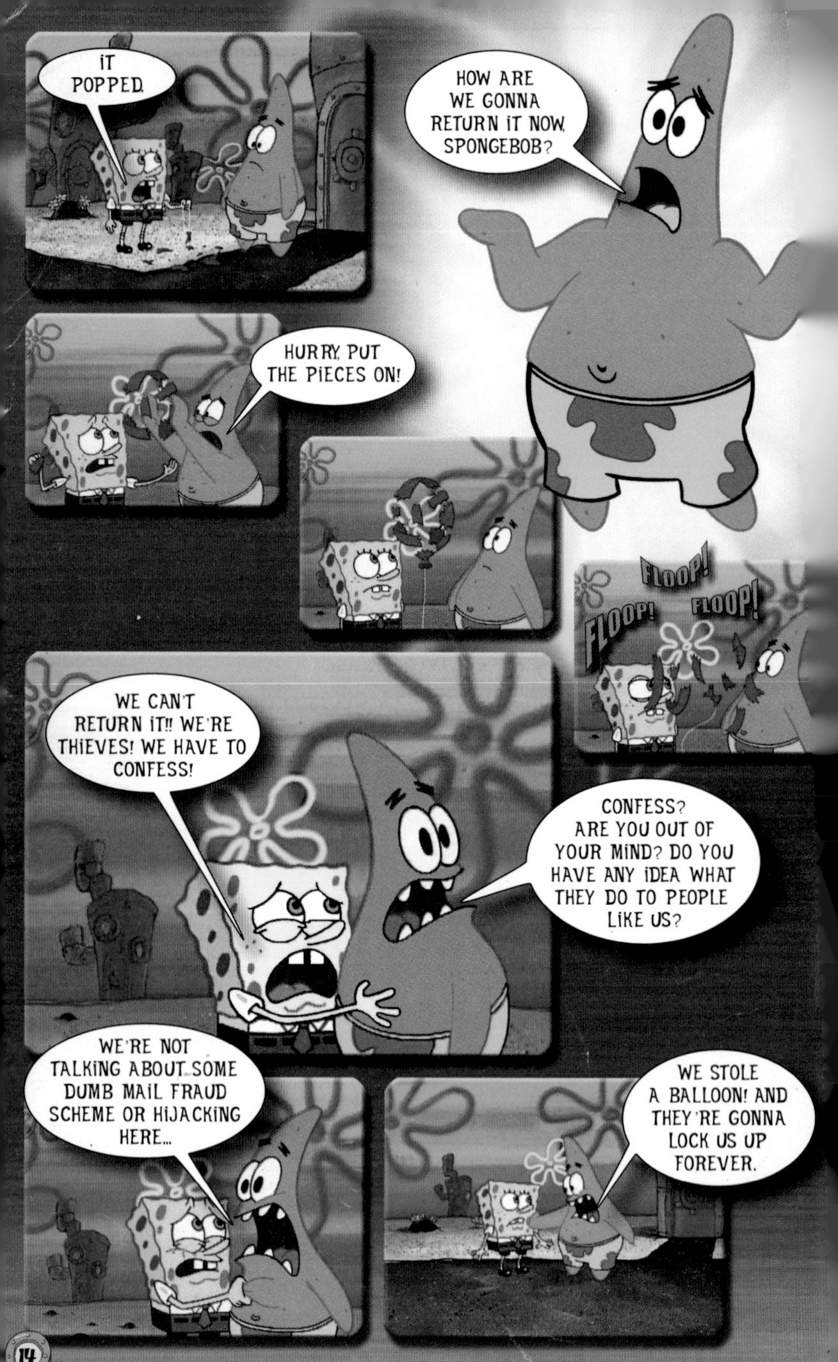
IT POPPED.
HOW ARE WE GONNA RETURN IT NOW, SPONGEBOB?
HURRY, PUT THE PIECES ON!
FLOOP!
FLOOP!
FLOOP!
WE CAN'T RETURN IT!! WE'RE THIEVES! WE HAVE TO CONFESS!
CONFESS? ARE YOU OUT OF YOUR MIND? DO YOU HAVE ANY IDEA WHAT THEY DO TO PEOPLE LIKE US?
WE'RE NOT TALKING ABOUT SOME DUMB MAIL FRAUD SCHEME OR HIJACKING HERE...
WE STOLE A BALLOON! AND THEY'RE GONNA LOCK US UP FOREVER.

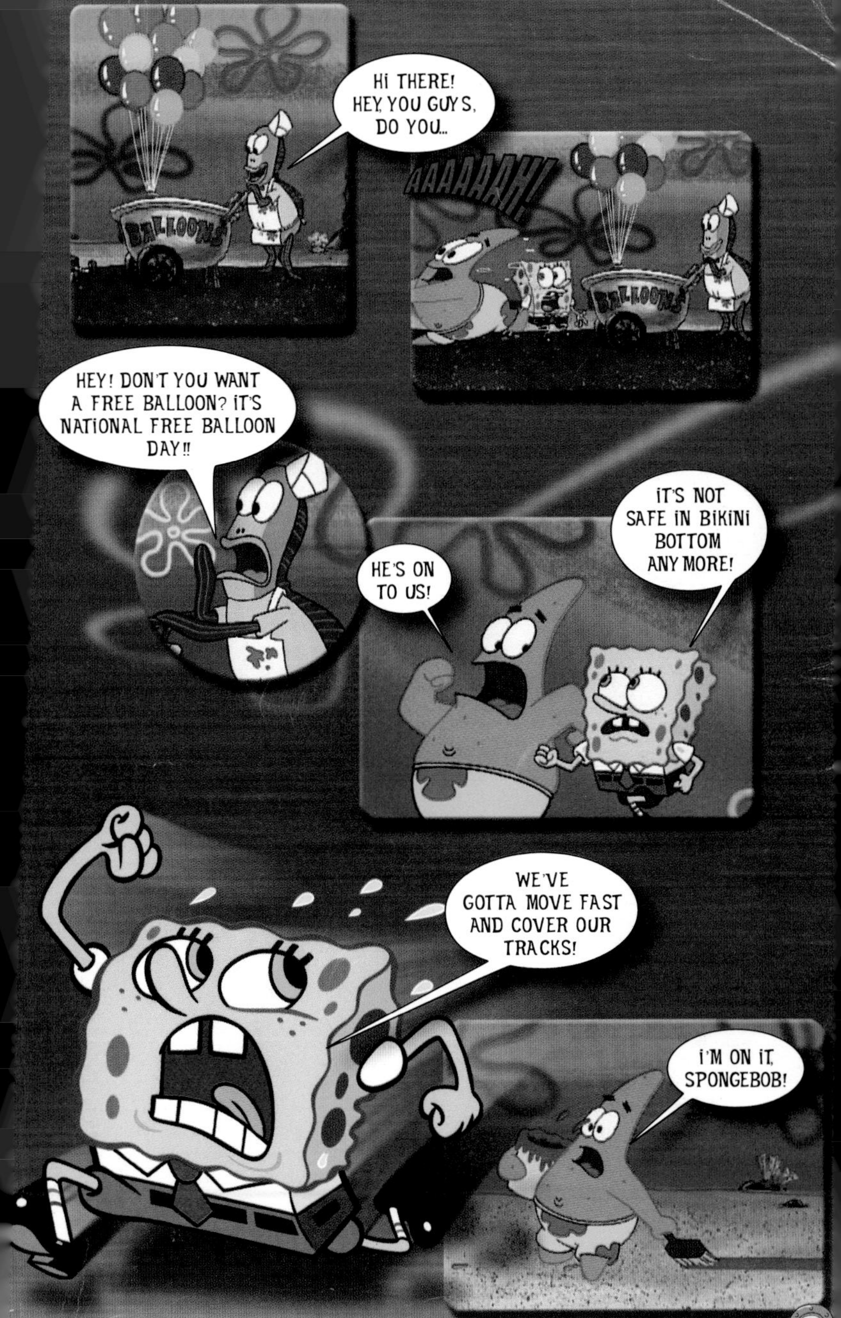
HI THERE! HEY, YOU GUYS, DO YOU...
AAAAAAH!
HEY! DON'T YOU WANT A FREE BALLOON? IT'S NATIONAL FREE BALLOON DAY!!
HE'S ON TO US!
IT'S NOT SAFE IN BIKINI BOTTOM ANY MORE!
WE'VE GOTTA MOVE FAST AND COVER OUR TRACKS!
I'M ON IT, SPONGEBOB!

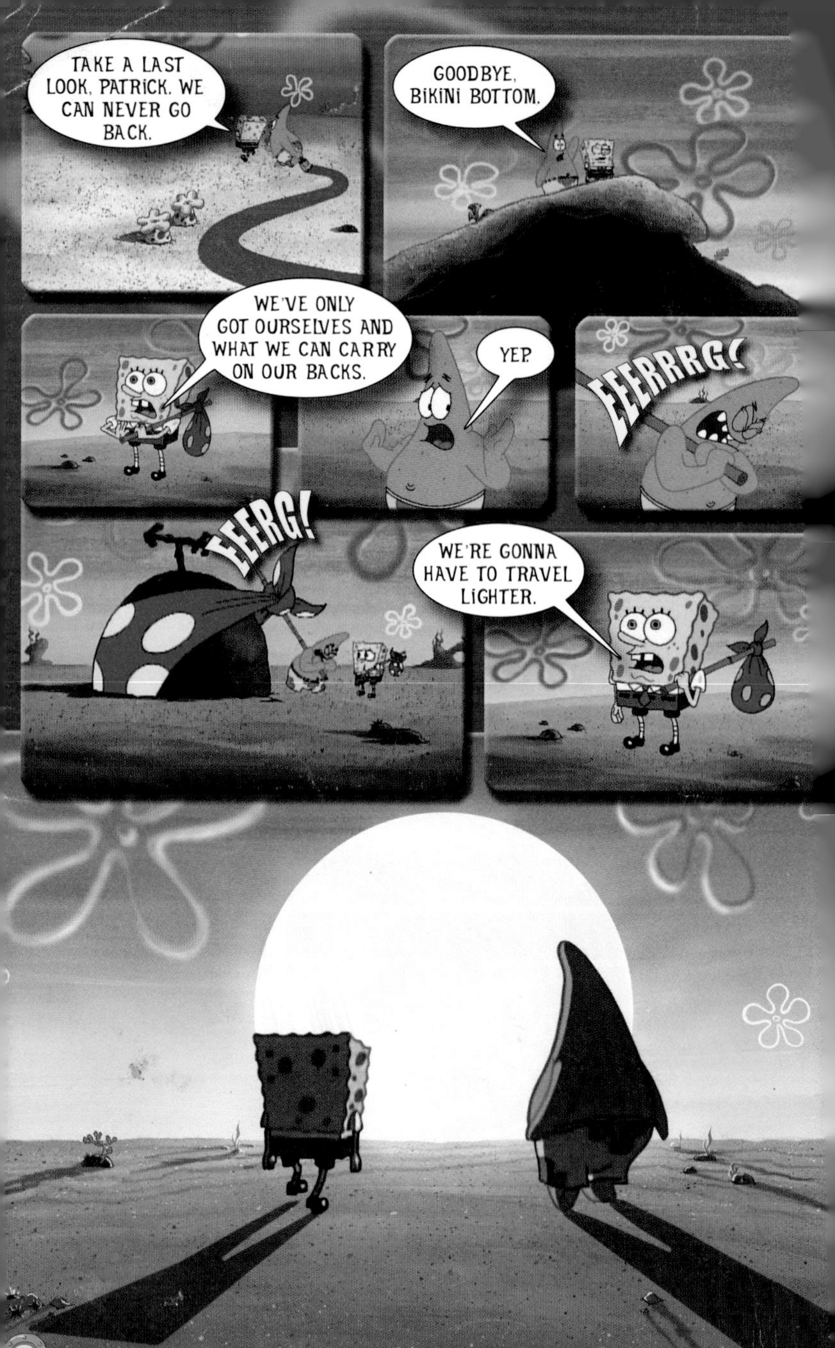
TAKE A LAST LOOK, PATRICK. WE CAN NEVER GO BACK.
GOODBYE, BIKINI BOTTOM.
WE'VE ONLY GOT OURSELVES AND WHAT WE CAN CARRY ON OUR BACKS.
YEP.
EEERRRG!
EEERG!
WE'RE GONNA HAVE TO TRAVEL LIGHTER.

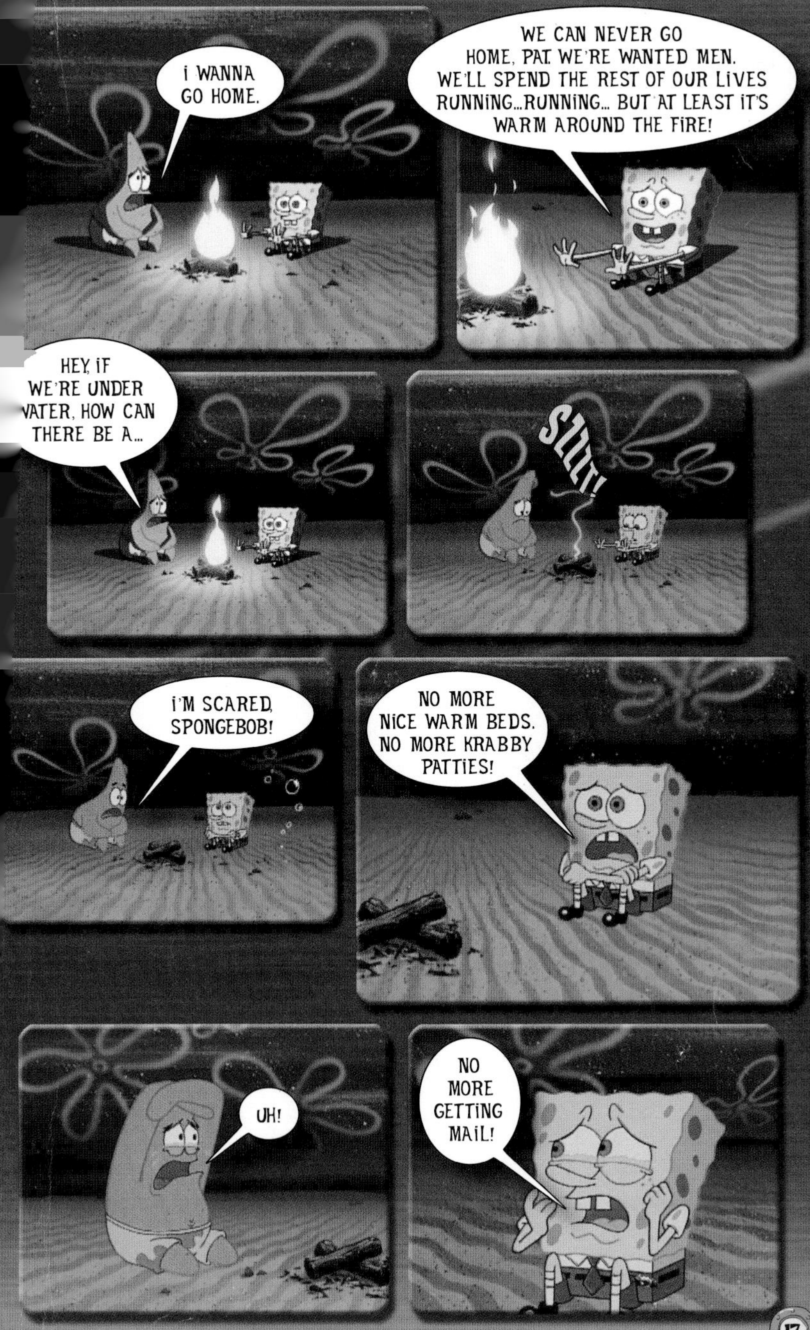
I WANNA GO HOME.
WE CAN NEVER GO HOME, PAT. WE'RE WANTED MEN. WE'LL SPEND THE REST OF OUR LIVES RUNNING...RUNNING... BUT AT LEAST IT'S WARM AROUND THE FIRE!
HEY, IF WE'RE UNDER WATER, HOW CAN THERE BE A...
SZZZT!
I'M SCARED, SPONGEBOB!
NO MORE NICE WARM BEDS. NO MORE KRABBY PATTIES!
UH!
NO MORE GETTING MAIL!

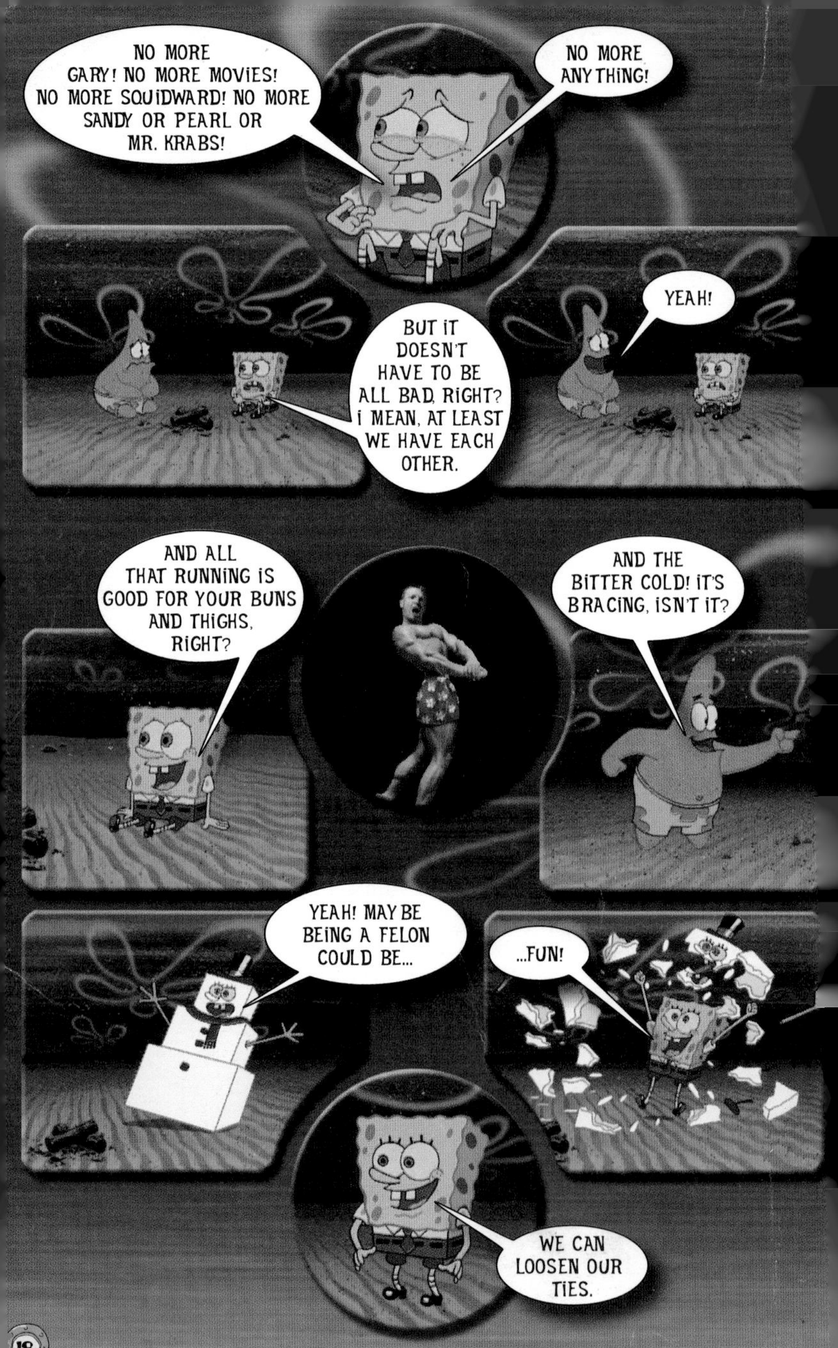
NO MORE GARY! NO MORE MOVIES! NO MORE SQUIDWARD! NO MORE SANDY OR PEARL OR MR. KRABS!
NO MORE ANYTHING!
BUT IT DOESN'T HAVE TO BE ALL BAD, RIGHT? I MEAN, AT LEAST WE HAVE EACH OTHER.
YEAH!
AND ALL THAT RUNNING IS GOOD FOR YOUR BUNS AND THIGHS, RIGHT?
AND THE BITTER COLD! IT'S BRACING, ISN'T IT?
YEAH! MAYBE BEING A FELON COULD BE...
...FUN!
WE CAN LOOSEN OUR TIES.

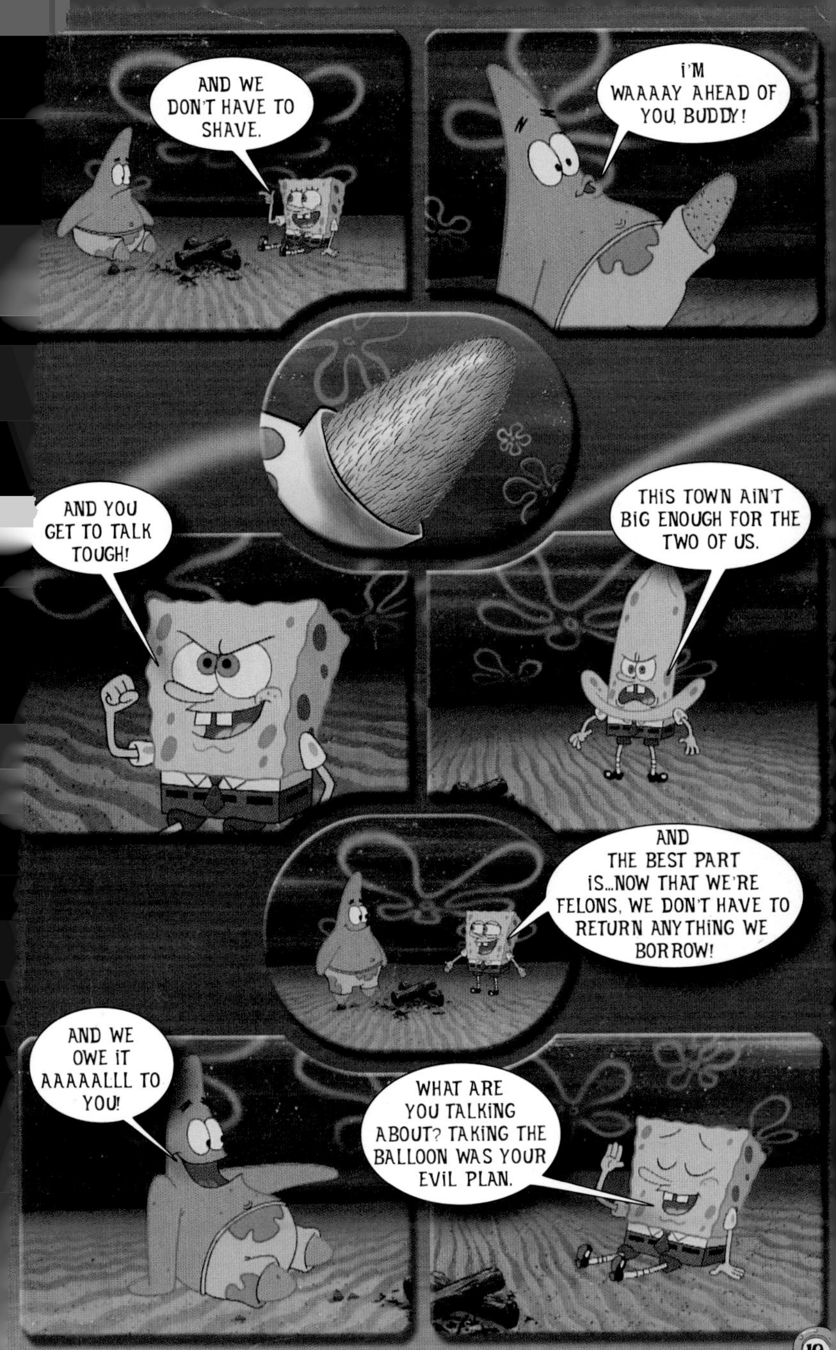
AND WE DON'T HAVE TO SHAVE.
I'M WAAAAY AHEAD OF YOU, BUDDY!
AND YOU GET TO TALK TOUGH!
THIS TOWN AIN'T BIG ENOUGH FOR THE TWO OF US.
AND THE BEST PART IS...NOW THAT WE'RE FELONS, WE DON'T HAVE TO RETURN ANYTHING WE BORROW!
AND WE OWE IT AAAAALLL TO YOU!
WHAT ARE YOU TALKING ABOUT? TAKING THE BALLOON WAS YOUR EVIL PLAN.

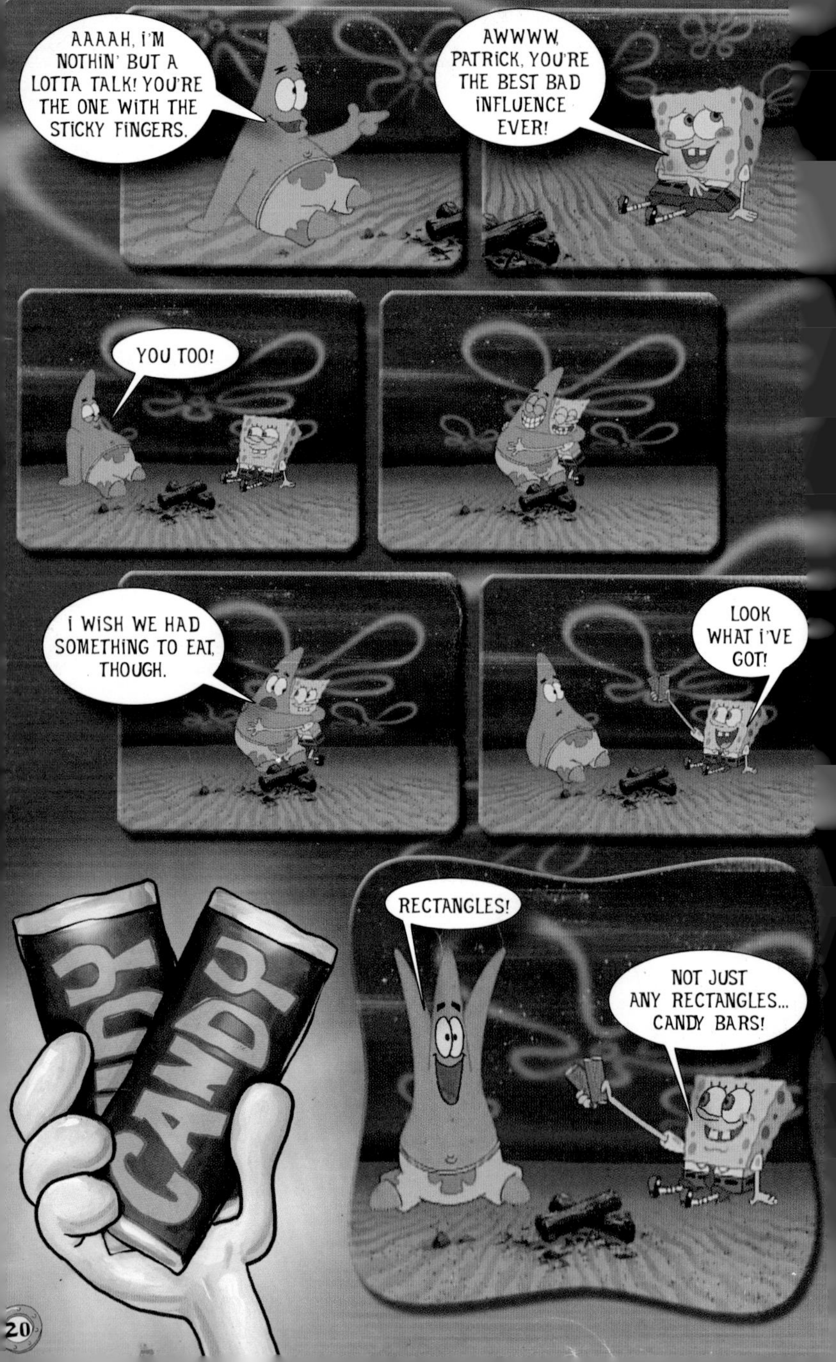
AAAAH, I'M NOTHIN' BUT A LOTTA TALK! YOU'RE THE ONE WITH THE STICKY FINGERS.
AWWWW, PATRICK, YOU'RE THE BEST BAD INFLUENCE EVER!
YOU TOO!
I WISH WE HAD SOMETHING TO EAT, THOUGH.
LOOK WHAT I'VE GOT!
CANDY
CANDY
RECTANGLES!
NOT JUST ANY RECTANGLES... CANDY BARS!

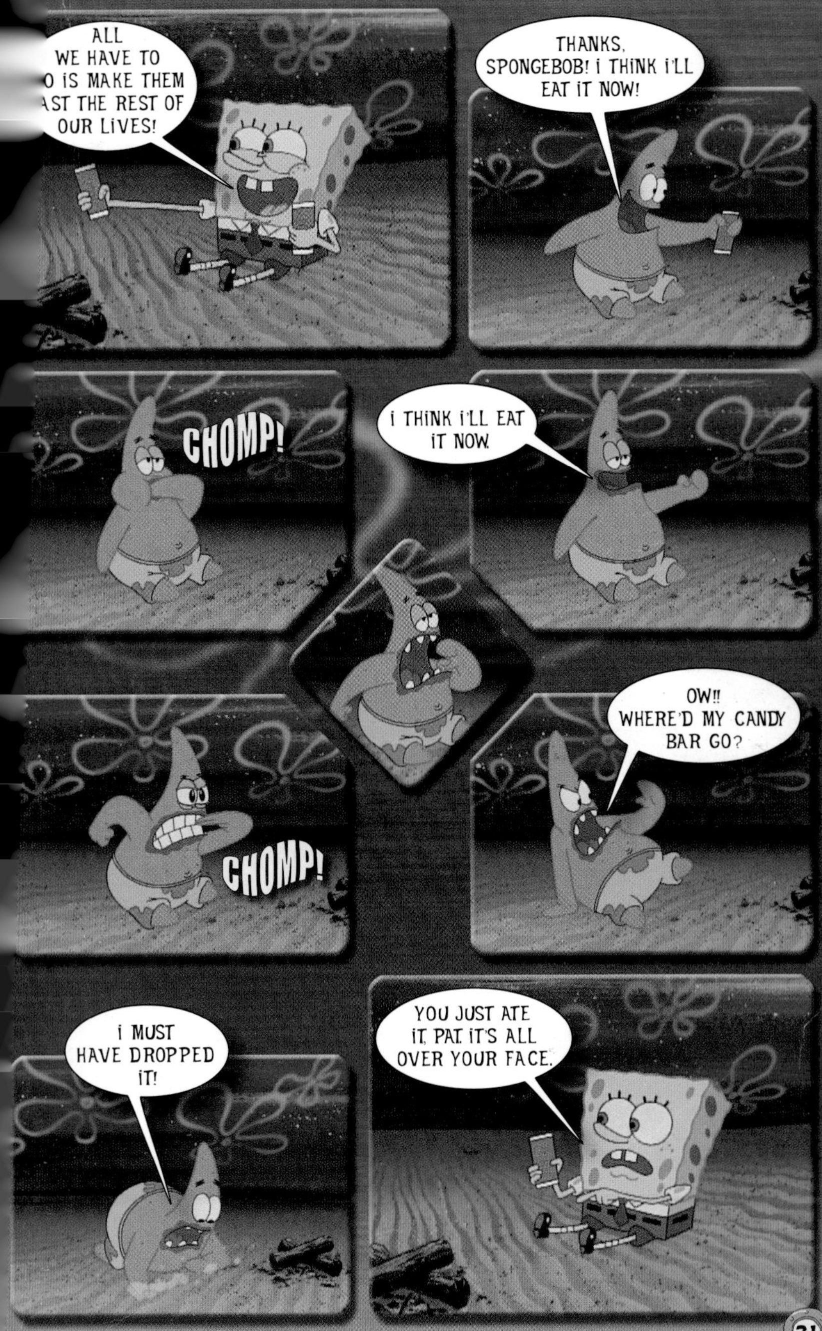
ALL WE HAVE TO O IS MAKE THEM AST THE REST OF OUR LIVES!
THANKS, SPONGEBOB! I THINK I'LL EAT IT NOW!
CHOMP!
I THINK I'LL EAT IT NOW.
CHOMP!
OW!! WHERE'D MY CANDY BAR GO?
I MUST HAVE DROPPED IT!
YOU JUST ATE IT, PAT. IT'S ALL OVER YOUR FACE.

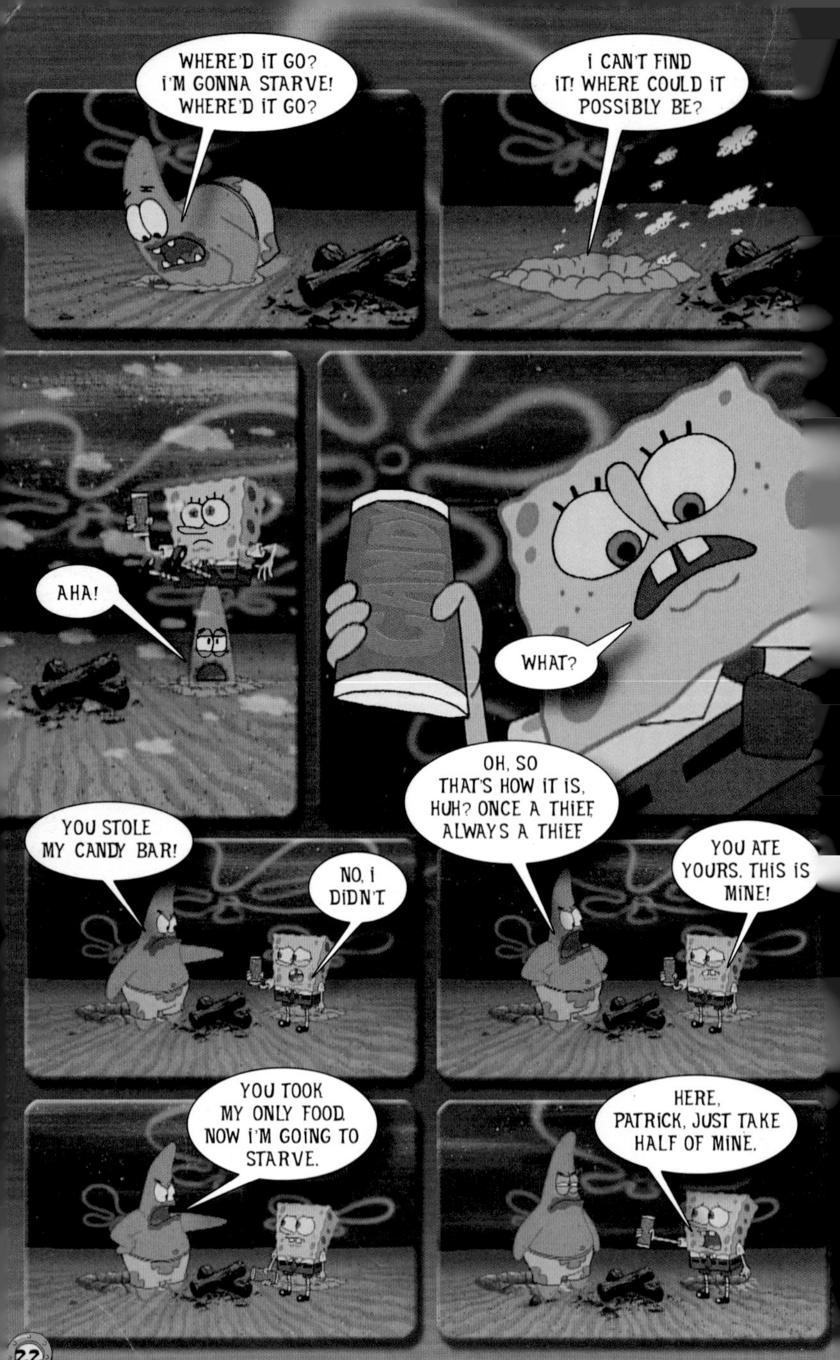
WHERE'D IT GO? I'M GONNA STARVE! WHERE'D IT GO?
I CAN'T FIND IT! WHERE COULD IT POSSIBLY BE?
AHA!
WHAT?
YOU STOLE MY CANDY BAR!
NO, I DIDN'T.
OH, SO THAT'S HOW IT IS, HUH? ONCE A THIEF, ALWAYS A THIEF.
YOU ATE YOURS. THIS IS MINE!
YOU TOOK MY ONLY FOOD. NOW I'M GOING TO STARVE.
HERE, PATRICK, JUST TAKE HALF OF MINE.

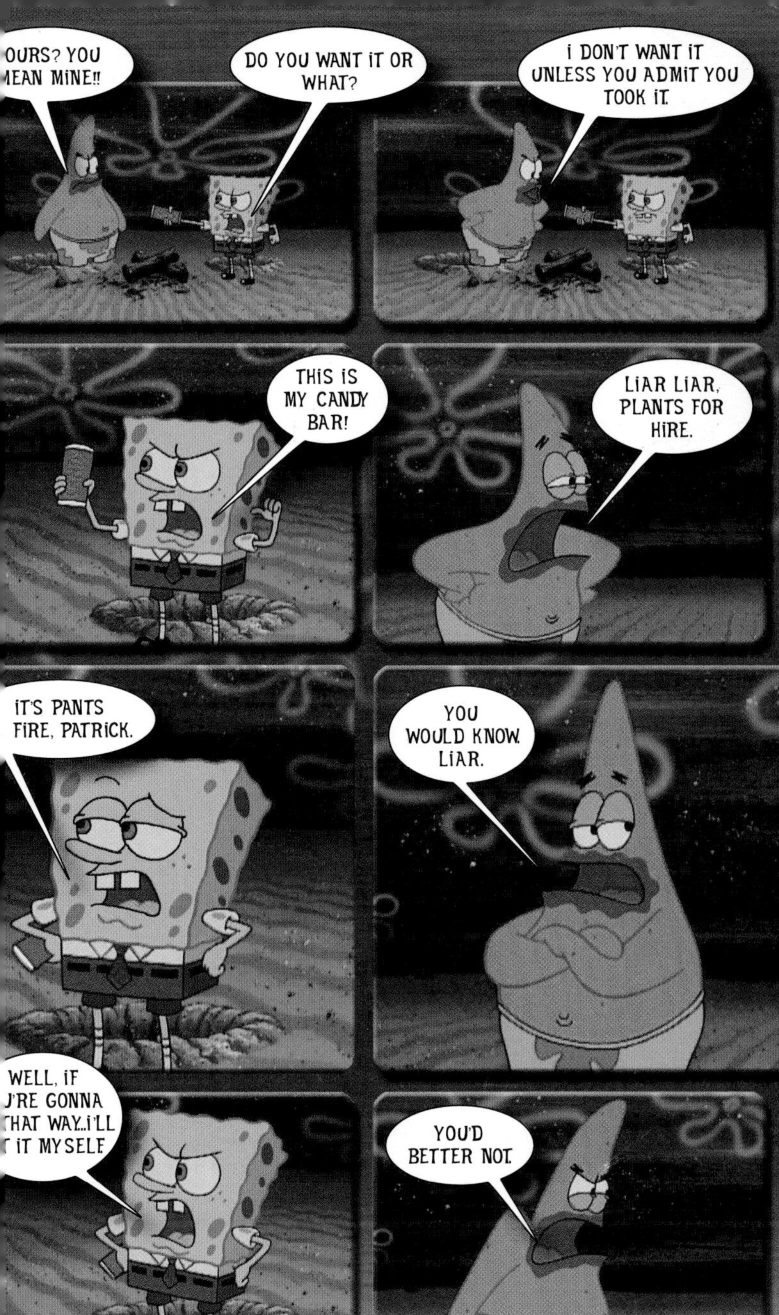
OURS? YOU
IEAN MINE!!
DO YOU WANT IT OR WHAT?
I DON'T WANT IT UNLESS YOU ADMIT YOU TOOK IT.
THIS IS MY CANDY BAR!
LIAR LIAR, PLANTS FOR HIRE.
IT'S PANTS
FIRE, PATRICK.
YOU WOULD KNOW. LIAR.
WELL, IF
J'RE GONNA
THAT WAY...I'LL
T IT MYSELF.
YOU'D BETTER NOT.

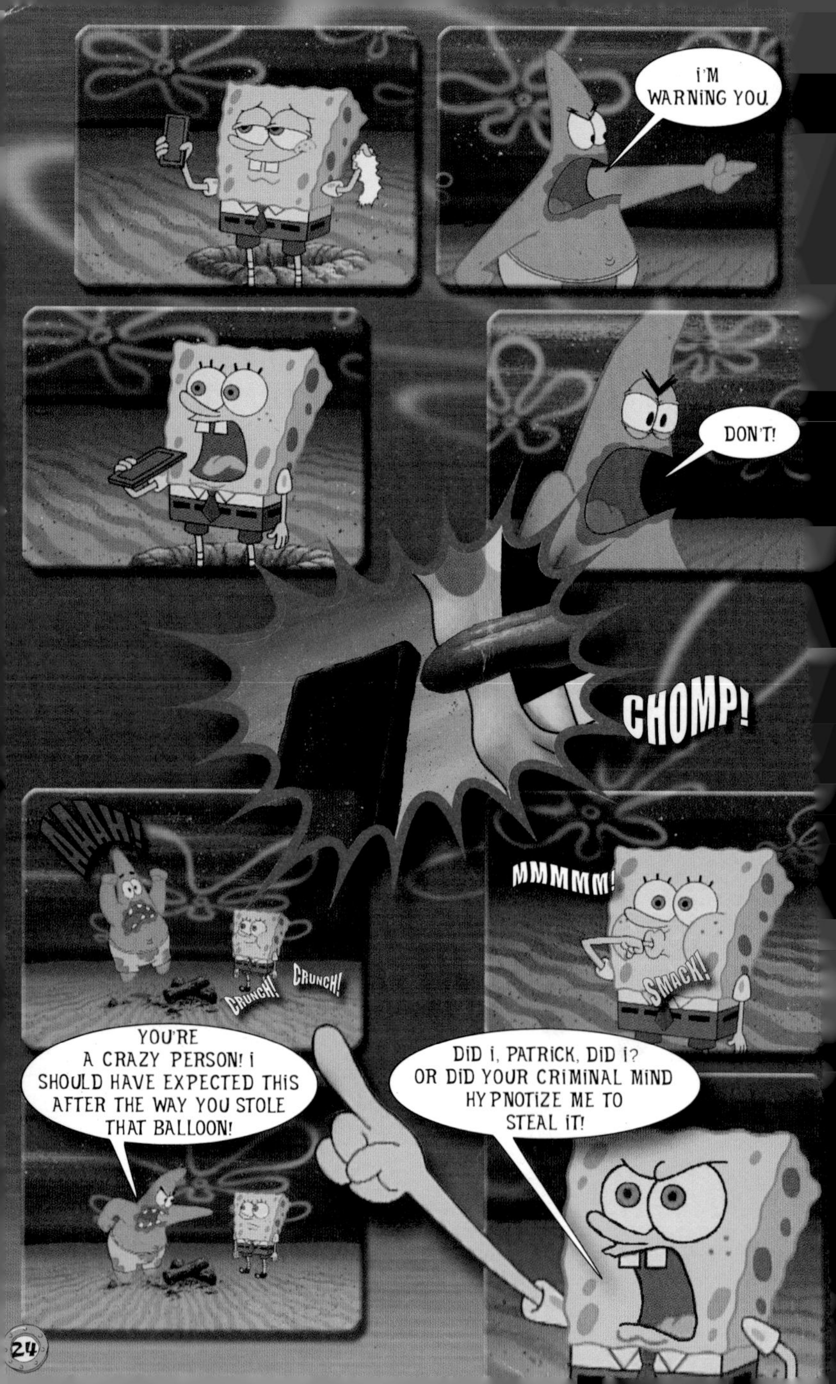
I'M WARNING YOU.
DON'T!
CHOMP!
AAAAH!
CRUNCH!
CRUNCH!
MMMMM!
SMACK!
YOU'RE A CRAZY PERSON! I SHOULD HAVE EXPECTED THIS AFTER THE WAY YOU STOLE THAT BALLOON!
DID I, PATRICK, DID I? OR DID YOUR CRIMINAL MIND HYPNOTIZE ME TO STEAL IT!

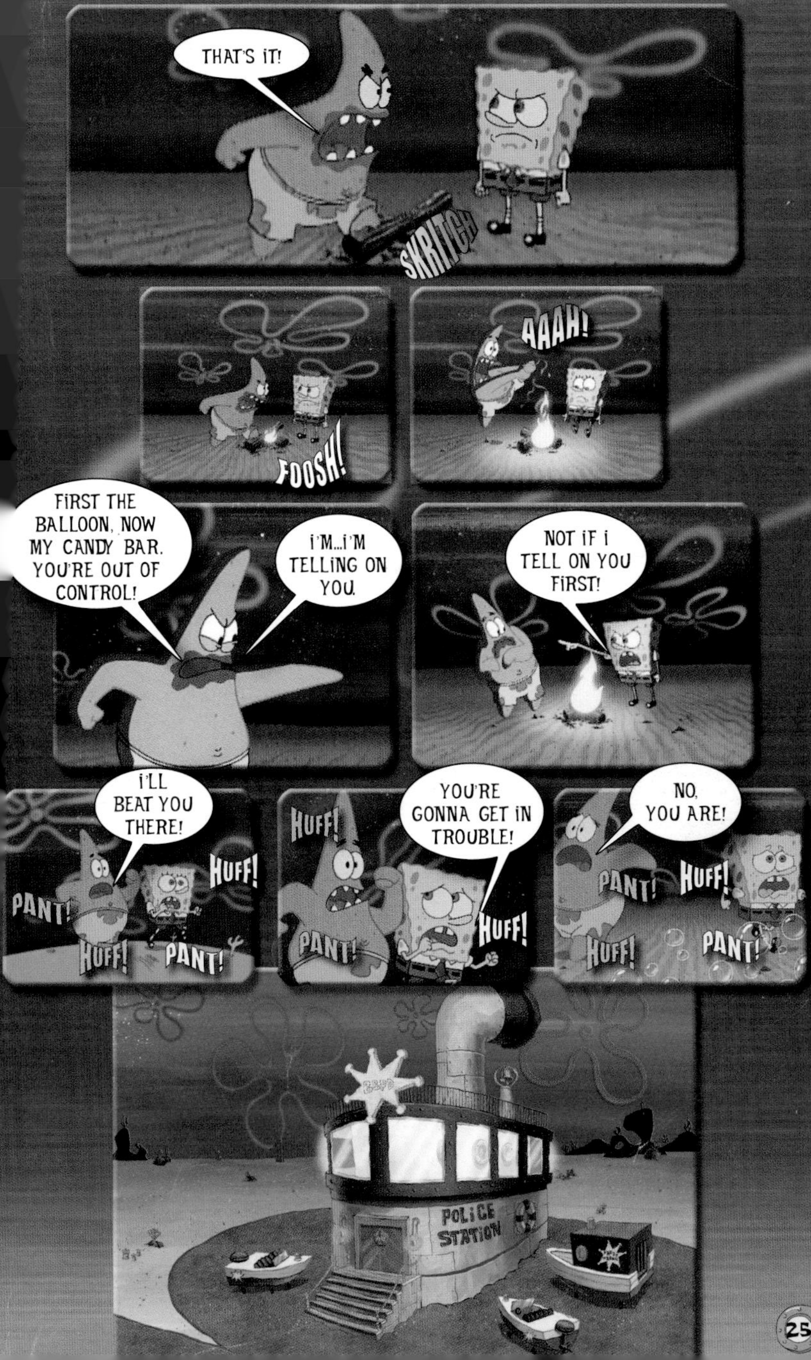

THAT'S IT!
SKRITCH
FOOSH!
AAAH!
FIRST THE BALLOON, NOW MY CANDY BAR. YOU'RE OUT OF CONTROL!
I'M...I'M TELLING ON YOU.
NOT IF I TELL ON YOU FIRST!
I'LL BEAT YOU THERE!
PANT!
HUFF!
HUFF!
PANT!
HUFF!
YOU'RE GONNA GET IN TROUBLE!
PANT!
HUFF!
NO, YOU ARE!
PANT!
HUFF!
HUFF!
PANT!
POLICE STATION

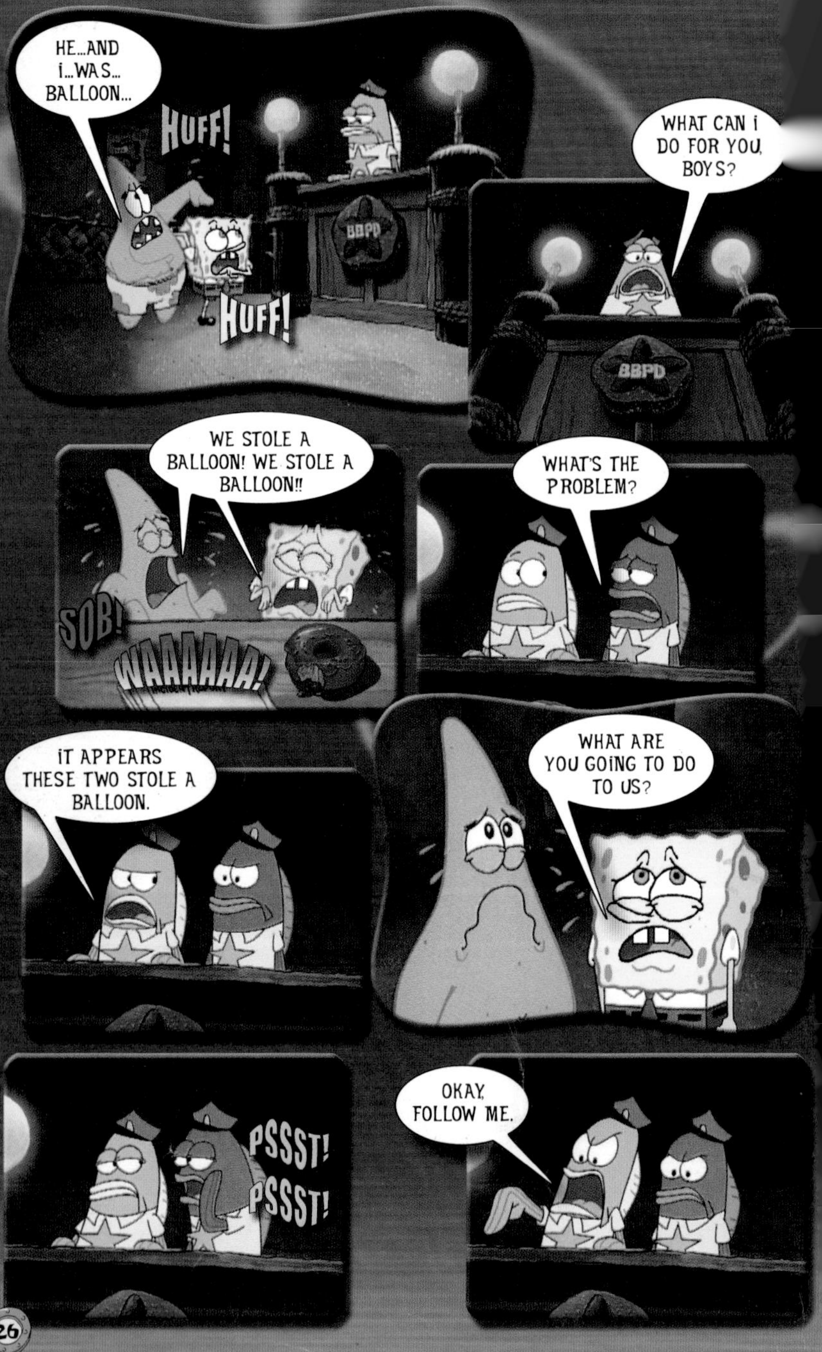
HE...AND I...WAS... BALLOON...
HUFF!
HUFF!
BBPD
WHAT CAN I DO FOR YOU, BOYS?
BBPD
WE STOLE A BALLOON! WE STOLE A BALLOON!!
SOB!
WAAAAAA!
WHAT'S THE PROBLEM?
IT APPEARS THESE TWO STOLE A BALLOON.
WHAT ARE YOU GOING TO DO TO US?
PSSST! PSSST!
OKAY, FOLLOW ME.

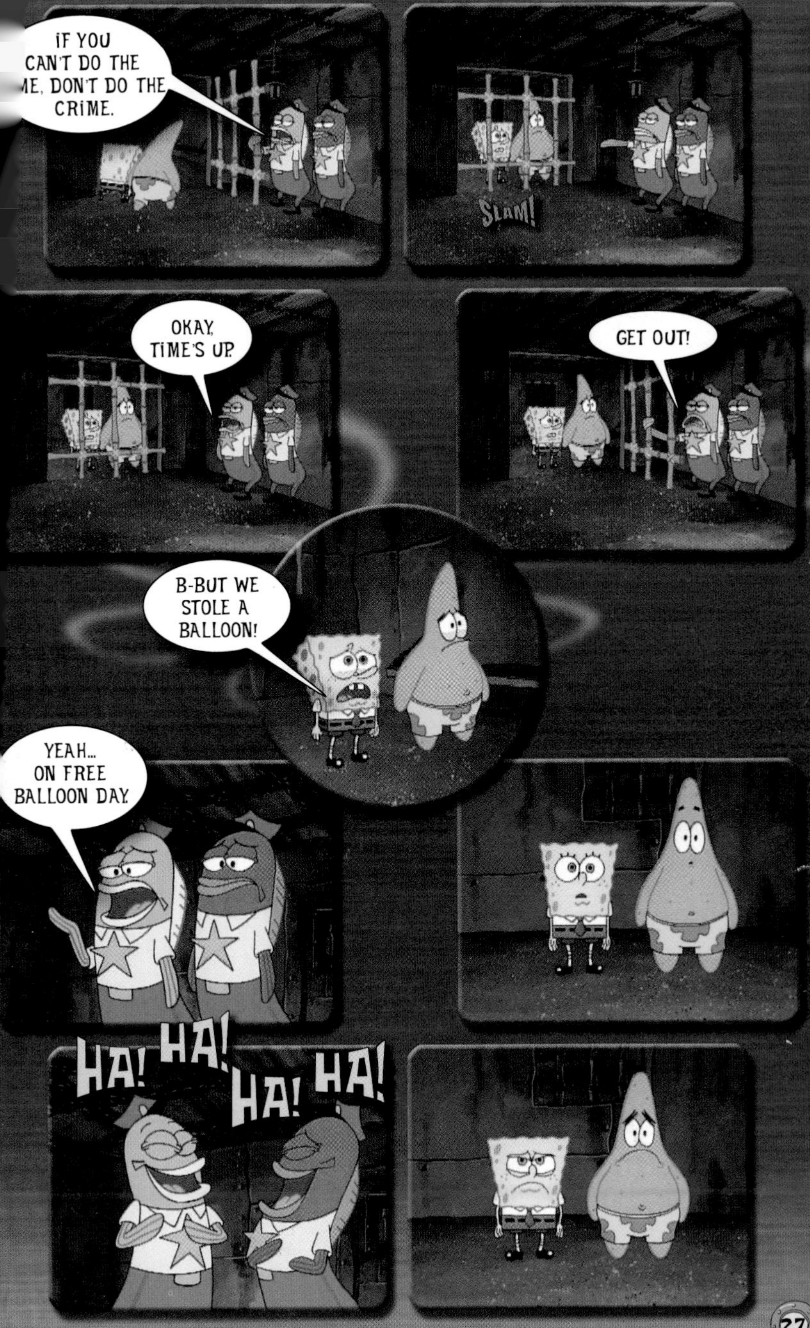
IF YOU CAN'T DO THE ME, DON'T DO THE CRIME.
SLAM!
OKAY, TIME'S UP.
GET OUT!
B-BUT WE STOLE A BALLOON!
YEAH... ON FREE BALLOON DAY.
HA! HA! HA! HA!

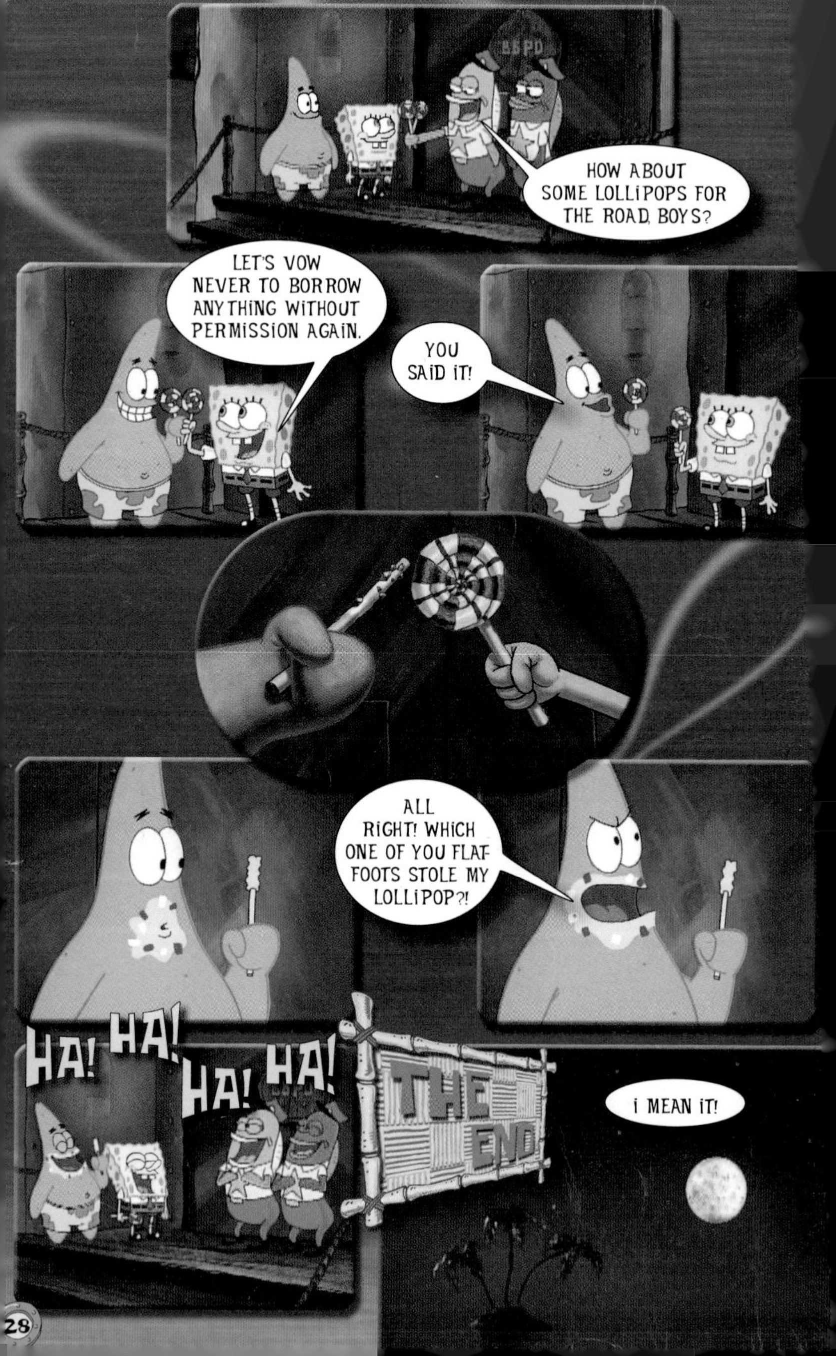
BBPD
HOW ABOUT SOME LOLLIPOPS FOR THE ROAD, BOYS?
LET'S VOW NEVER TO BORROW ANYTHING WITHOUT PERMISSION AGAIN.
YOU SAID IT!
ALL RIGHT! WHICH ONE OF YOU FLAT-FOOTS STOLE MY LOLLIPOP?!
HA! HA! HA! HA!
THE END
I MEAN IT!

SpongeBob SquarePants

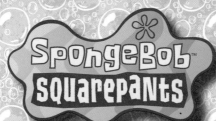

No Free Rides

by Aaron Springer, C. H. Greenblatt and Mr. Lawrence

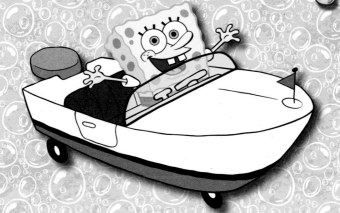

HERE WE ARE AGAIN AT THE BIKINI BOTTOM BOATING SCHOOL.

TODAY IS ONCE AGAIN THE DAY OF SPONGEBOB BOATING SCHOOL EXAM.

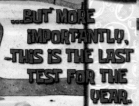

...BUT MORE IMPORTANTLY, -THIS IS THE LAST TEST FOR THE YEAR.

BEEP!

AND IF SPONGEBOB DOES NOT PASS THIS ONE, IT MEANS ANOTHER WHOLE YEAR OF BOATING SCHOOL!

AAAAAAAA!

KA-THUNK!

WHAT HAPPENED?

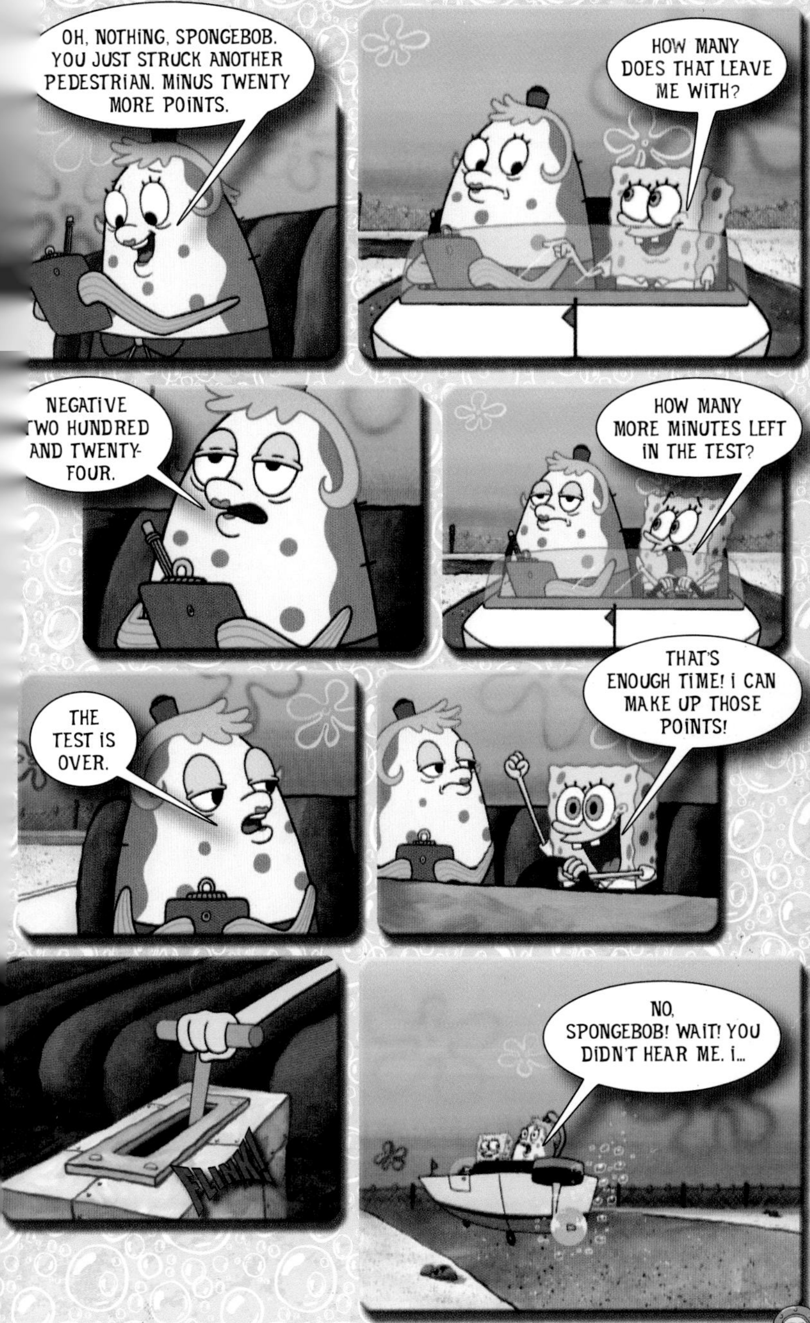
OH, NOTHING, SPONGEBOB. YOU JUST STRUCK ANOTHER PEDESTRIAN. MINUS TWENTY MORE POINTS.
HOW MANY DOES THAT LEAVE ME WITH?
NEGATIVE TWO HUNDRED AND TWENTY-FOUR.
HOW MANY MORE MINUTES LEFT IN THE TEST?
THE TEST IS OVER.
THAT'S ENOUGH TIME! I CAN MAKE UP THOSE POINTS!
FLUNK!
NO, SPONGEBOB! WAIT! YOU DIDN'T HEAR ME. I...

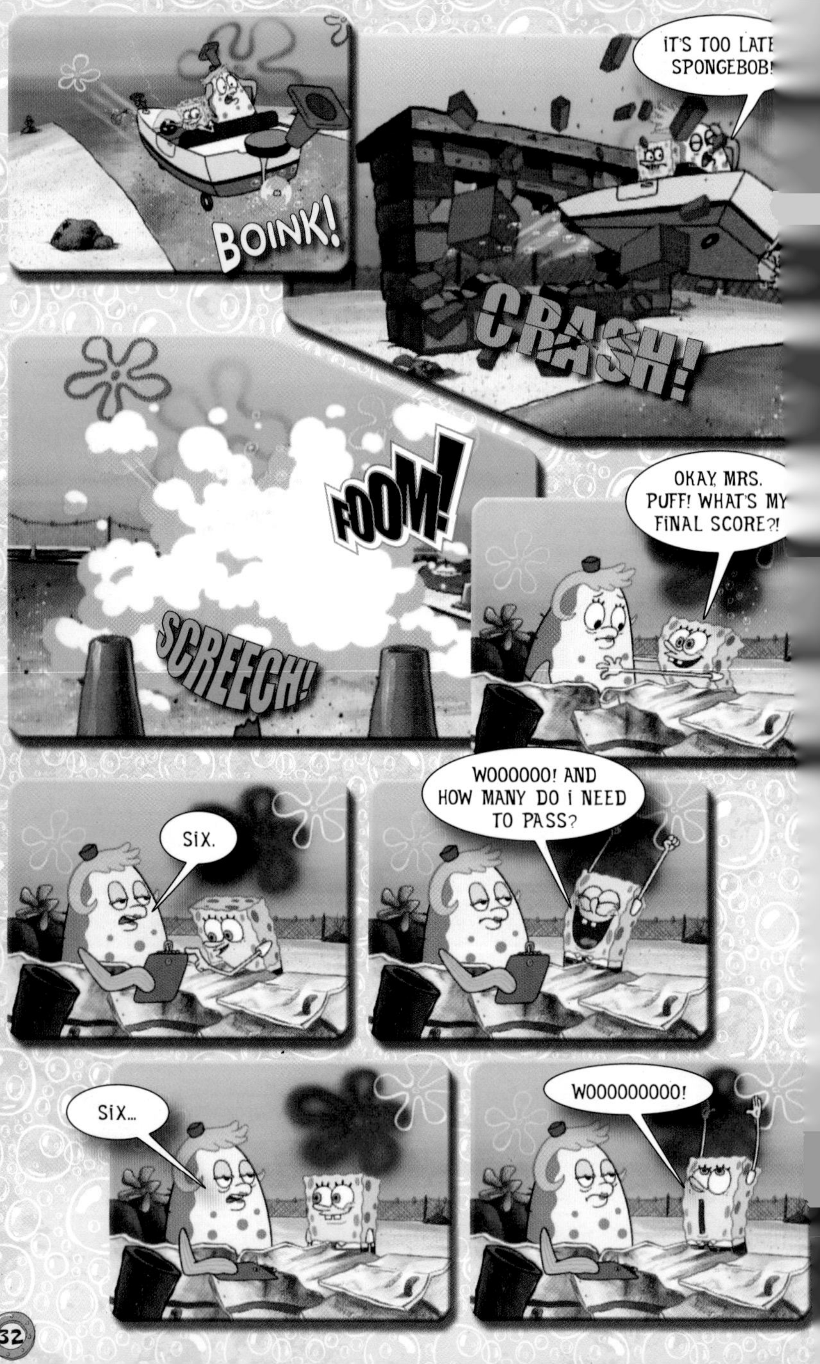
BOINK!
IT'S TOO LATE SPONGEBOB!
CRASH!
CRASH!
FOOM!
SCREECH!
OKAY, MRS. PUFF! WHAT'S MY FINAL SCORE?!
SIX.
WOOOOOO! AND HOW MANY DO I NEED TO PASS?
SIX...
WOOOOOOOOO!

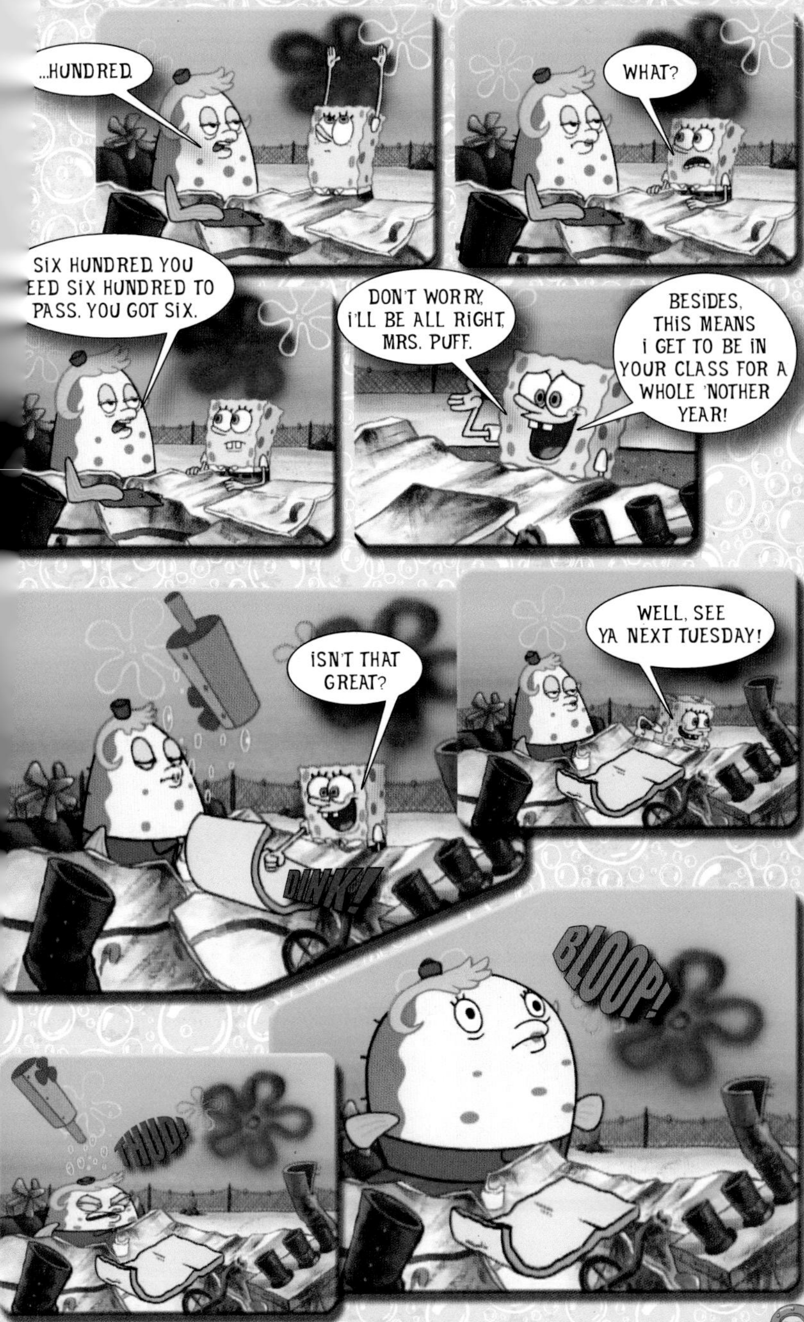
...HUNDRED.
WHAT?
SIX HUNDRED. YOU
EED SIX HUNDRED TO PASS. YOU GOT SIX.
DON'T WORRY, I'LL BE ALL RIGHT, MRS. PUFF.
BESIDES, THIS MEANS I GET TO BE IN YOUR CLASS FOR A WHOLE 'NOTHER YEAR!
ISN'T THAT GREAT?
DINK!!
WELL, SEE YA NEXT TUESDAY!
BLOOP!
THUD!

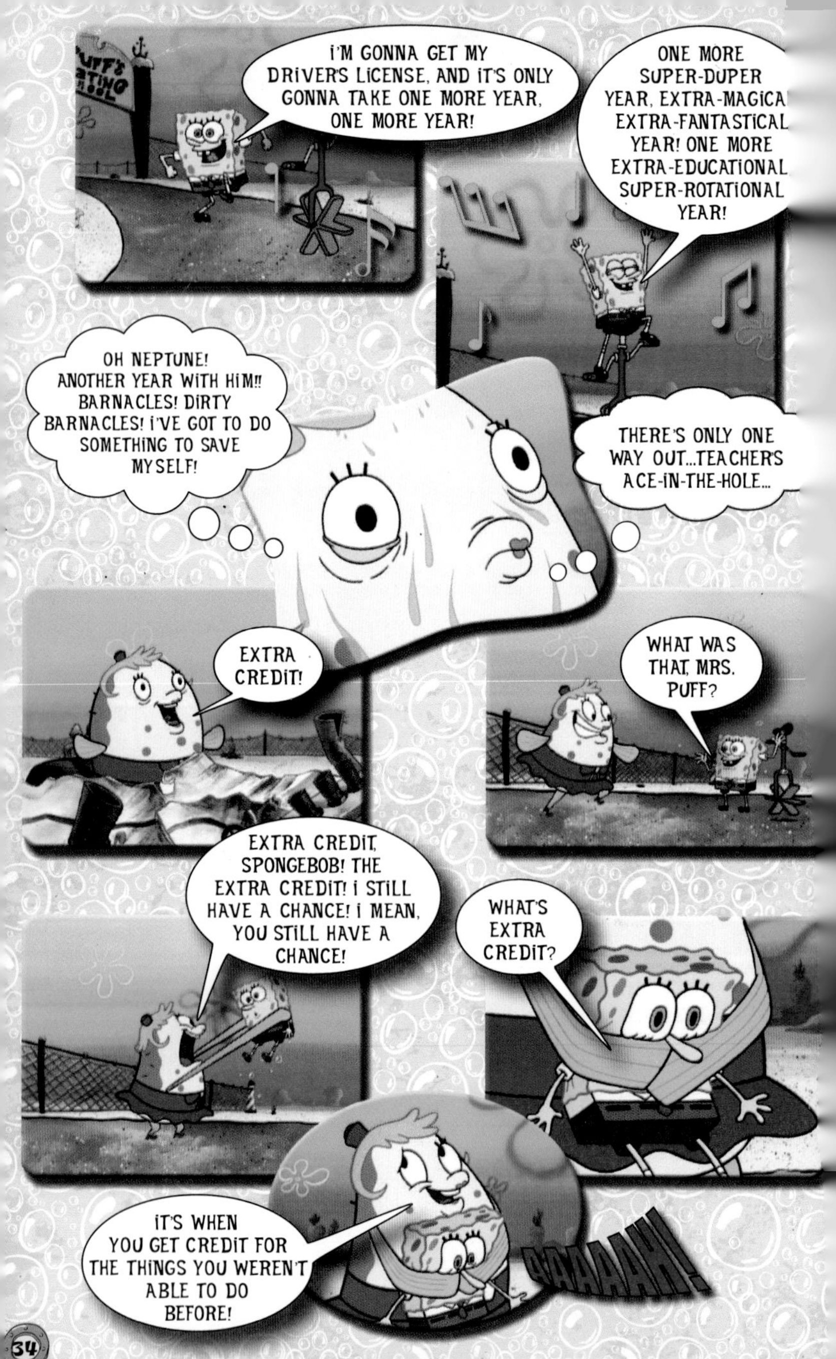
I'M GONNA GET MY DRIVER'S LICENSE, AND IT'S ONLY GONNA TAKE ONE MORE YEAR, ONE MORE YEAR!
ONE MORE SUPER-DUPER YEAR, EXTRA-MAGICAL EXTRA-FANTASTICAL YEAR! ONE MORE EXTRA-EDUCATIONAL SUPER-ROTATIONAL YEAR!
OH NEPTUNE! ANOTHER YEAR WITH HIM!! BARNACLES! DIRTY BARNACLES! I'VE GOT TO DO SOMETHING TO SAVE MYSELF!
THERE'S ONLY ONE WAY OUT...TEACHER'S ACE-IN-THE-HOLE...
EXTRA CREDIT!
WHAT WAS THAT, MRS. PUFF?
EXTRA CREDIT, SPONGEBOB! THE EXTRA CREDIT! I STILL HAVE A CHANCE! I MEAN, YOU STILL HAVE A CHANCE!
WHAT'S EXTRA CREDIT?
IT'S WHEN YOU GET CREDIT FOR THE THINGS YOU WEREN'T ABLE TO DO BEFORE!
AAAAAH!

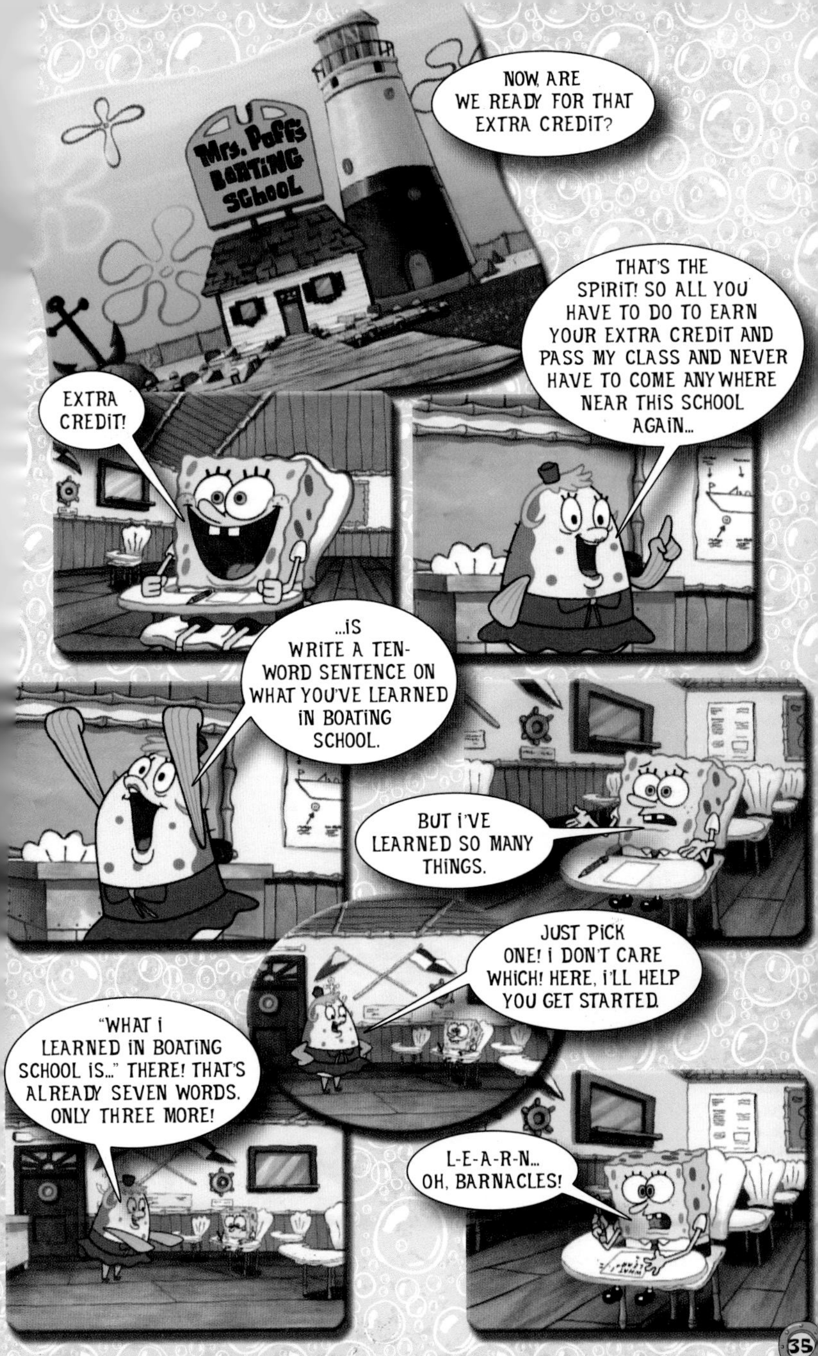
Mrs. Puff's BOATING SCHOOL
NOW, ARE WE READY FOR THAT EXTRA CREDIT?
EXTRA CREDIT!
THAT'S THE SPIRIT! SO ALL YOU HAVE TO DO TO EARN YOUR EXTRA CREDIT AND PASS MY CLASS AND NEVER HAVE TO COME ANYWHERE NEAR THIS SCHOOL AGAIN...
...IS WRITE A TEN-WORD SENTENCE ON WHAT YOU'VE LEARNED IN BOATING SCHOOL.
BUT I'VE LEARNED SO MANY THINGS.
JUST PICK ONE! I DON'T CARE WHICH! HERE, I'LL HELP YOU GET STARTED.
"WHAT I LEARNED IN BOATING SCHOOL IS..." THERE! THAT'S ALREADY SEVEN WORDS. ONLY THREE MORE!
L-E-A-R-N... OH, BARNACLES!

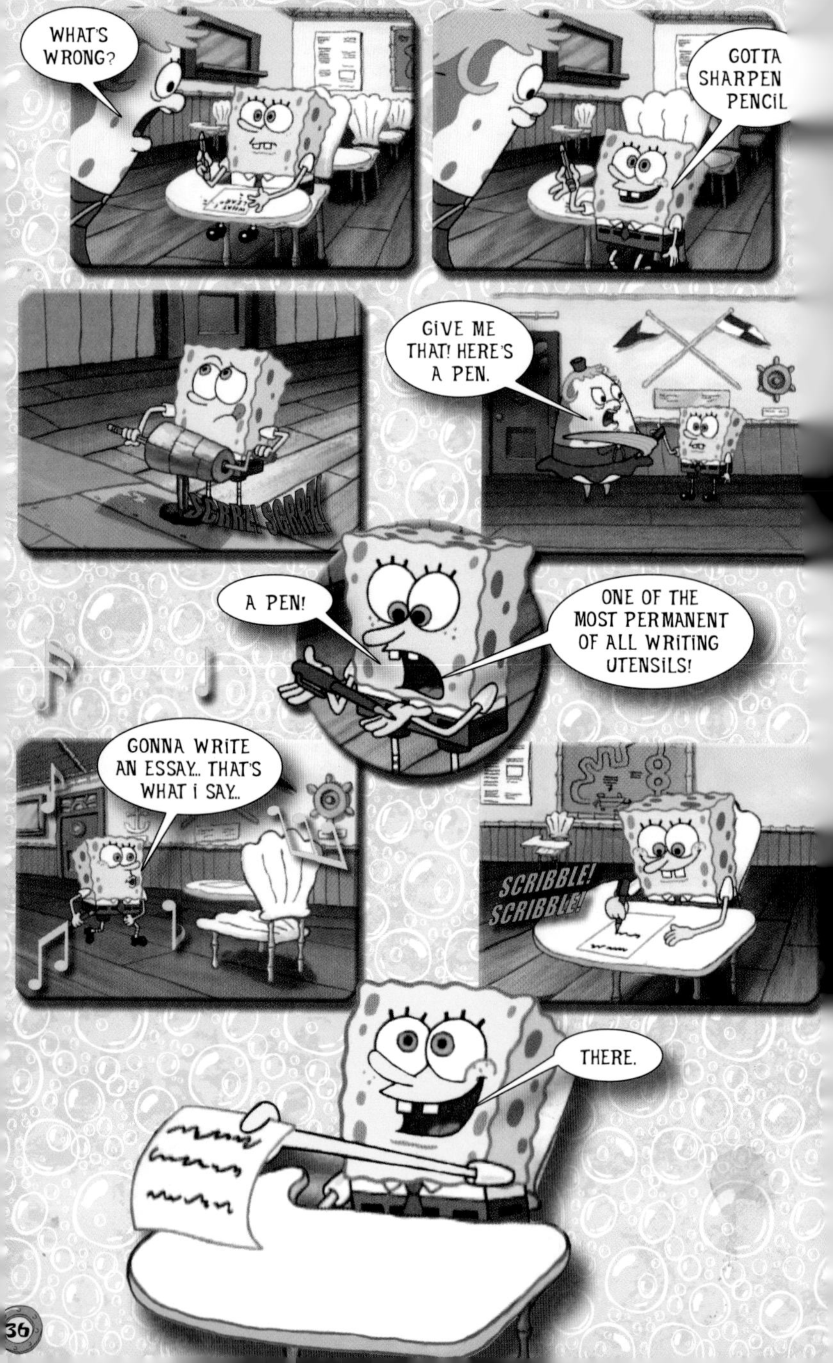
WHAT'S WRONG?
GOTTA SHARPEN PENCIL
GIVE ME THAT! HERE'S A PEN.
A PEN!
ONE OF THE MOST PERMANENT OF ALL WRITING UTENSILS!
GONNA WRITE AN ESSAY... THAT'S WHAT I SAY...
SCRIBBLE! SCRIBBLE!
THERE.

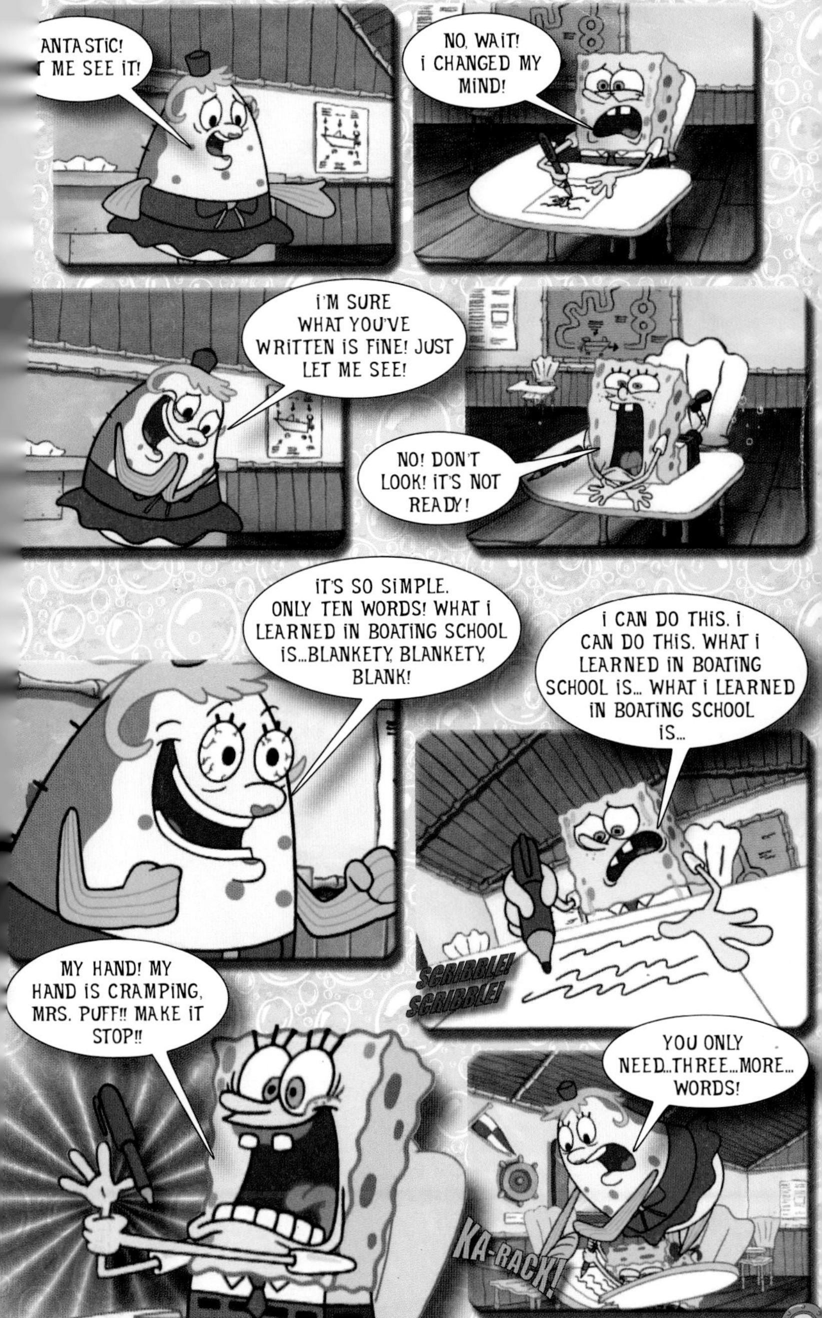
ANTASTIC! T ME SEE IT!
NO, WAIT! I CHANGED MY MIND!
I'M SURE WHAT YOU'VE WRITTEN IS FINE! JUST LET ME SEE!
NO! DON'T LOOK! IT'S NOT READY!
IT'S SO SIMPLE. ONLY TEN WORDS! WHAT I LEARNED IN BOATING SCHOOL IS...BLANKETY, BLANKETY, BLANK!
I CAN DO THIS. I CAN DO THIS. WHAT I LEARNED IN BOATING SCHOOL IS... WHAT I LEARNED IN BOATING SCHOOL IS...
SCRIBBLE! SCRIBBLE!
MY HAND! MY HAND IS CRAMPING, MRS. PUFF!! MAKE IT STOP!!
YOU ONLY NEED...THREE...MORE... WORDS!
KA-RACK!

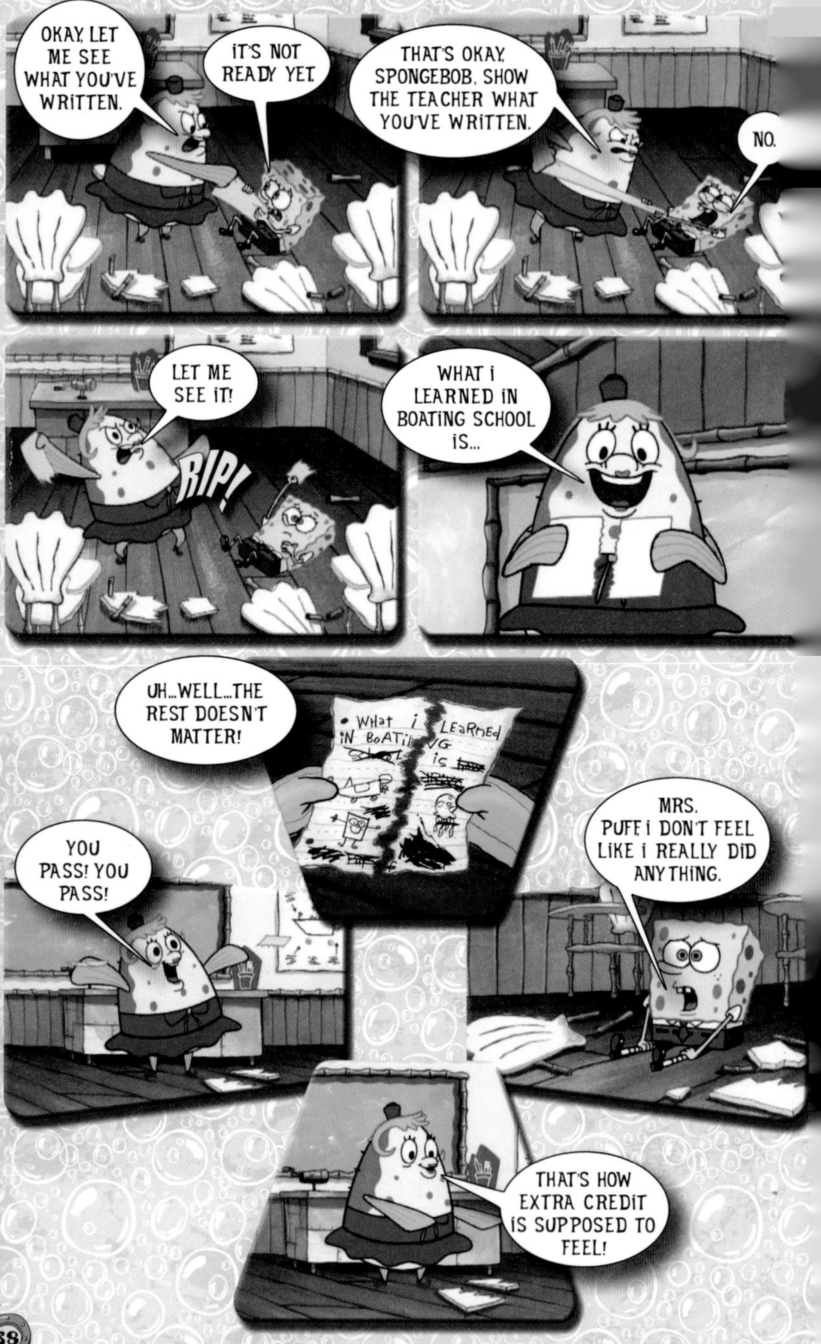
OKAY, LET ME SEE WHAT YOU'VE WRITTEN.
IT'S NOT READY YET.
THAT'S OKAY, SPONGEBOB, SHOW THE TEACHER WHAT YOU'VE WRITTEN.
NO.
LET ME SEE IT!
RIP!
WHAT I LEARNED IN BOATING SCHOOL IS...
UH...WELL...THE REST DOESN'T MATTER!
YOU PASS! YOU PASS!
MRS. PUFF, I DON'T FEEL LIKE I REALLY DID ANYTHING.
THAT'S HOW EXTRA CREDIT IS SUPPOSED TO FEEL!

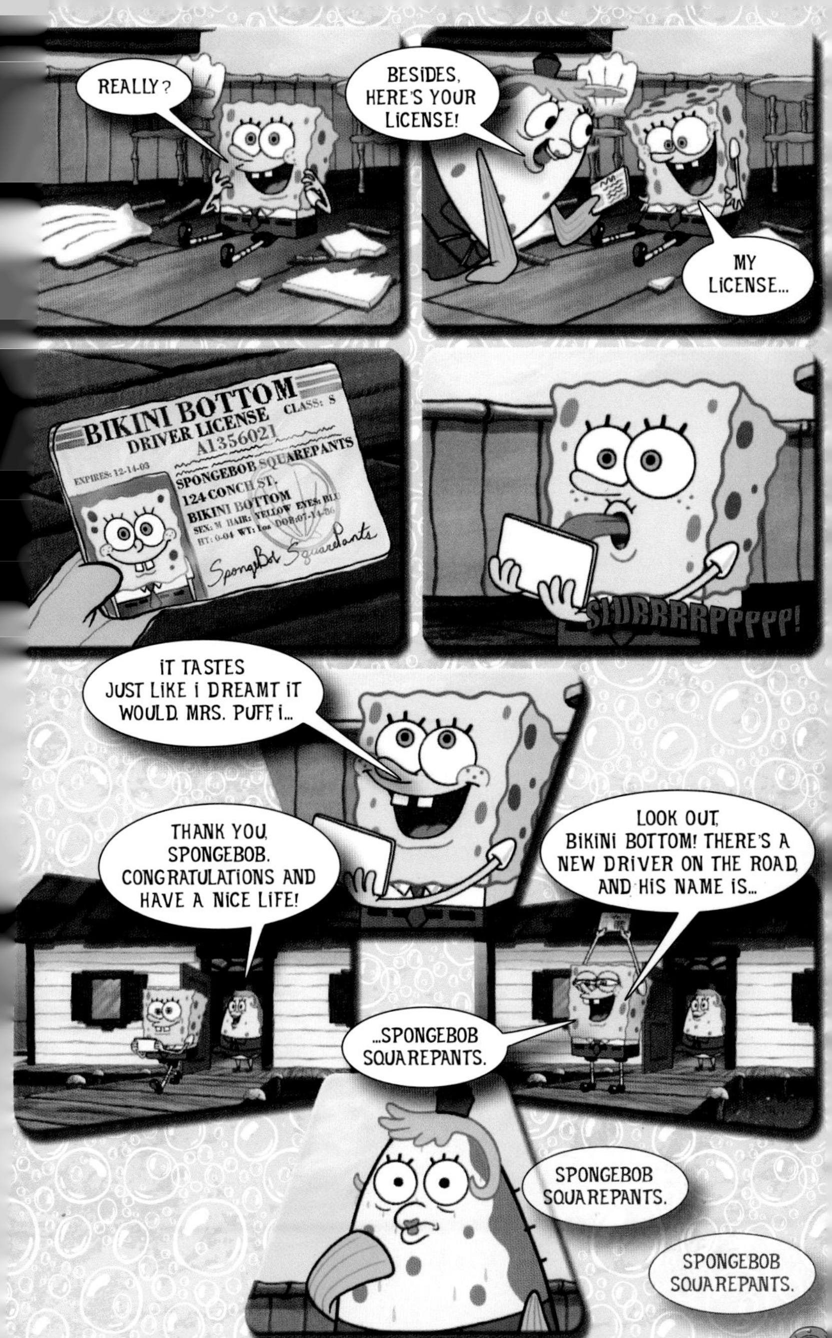

REALLY?
BESIDES, HERE'S YOUR LICENSE!
MY LICENSE...
BIKINI BOTTOM
DRIVER LICENSE
CLASS: S
A1356021
EXPIRES: 12-14-03
SPONGEBOB SQUAREPANTS
124 CONCH ST.
BIKINI BOTTOM
SLURRRRPPPPP!
IT TASTES JUST LIKE I DREAMT IT WOULD. MRS. PUFF, I...
THANK YOU, SPONGEBOB. CONGRATULATIONS AND HAVE A NICE LIFE!
LOOK OUT, BIKINI BOTTOM! THERE'S A NEW DRIVER ON THE ROAD, AND HIS NAME IS...
...SPONGEBOB SQUAREPANTS.
SPONGEBOB SQUAREPANTS.
SPONGEBOB SQUAREPANTS.

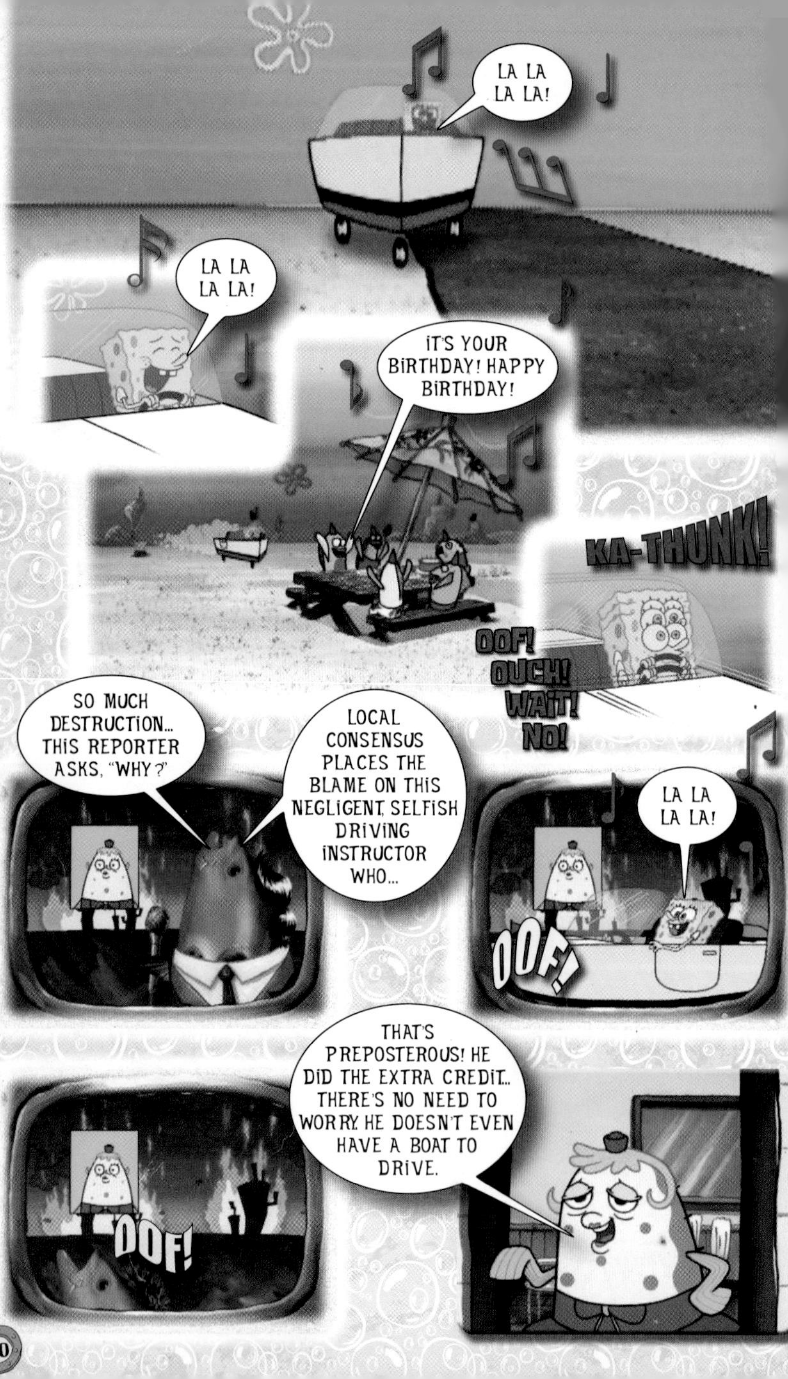
LA LA LA LA!
LA LA LA LA!
IT'S YOUR BIRTHDAY! HAPPY BIRTHDAY!
KA-THUNK!
OOF! OUCH! WAIT! NO!
SO MUCH DESTRUCTION... THIS REPORTER ASKS, "WHY?"
LOCAL CONSENSUS PLACES THE BLAME ON THIS NEGLIGENT, SELFISH DRIVING INSTRUCTOR WHO...
LA LA LA LA!
OOF!
OOF!
THAT'S PREPOSTEROUS! HE DID THE EXTRA CREDIT... THERE'S NO NEED TO WORRY. HE DOESN'T EVEN HAVE A BOAT TO DRIVE.

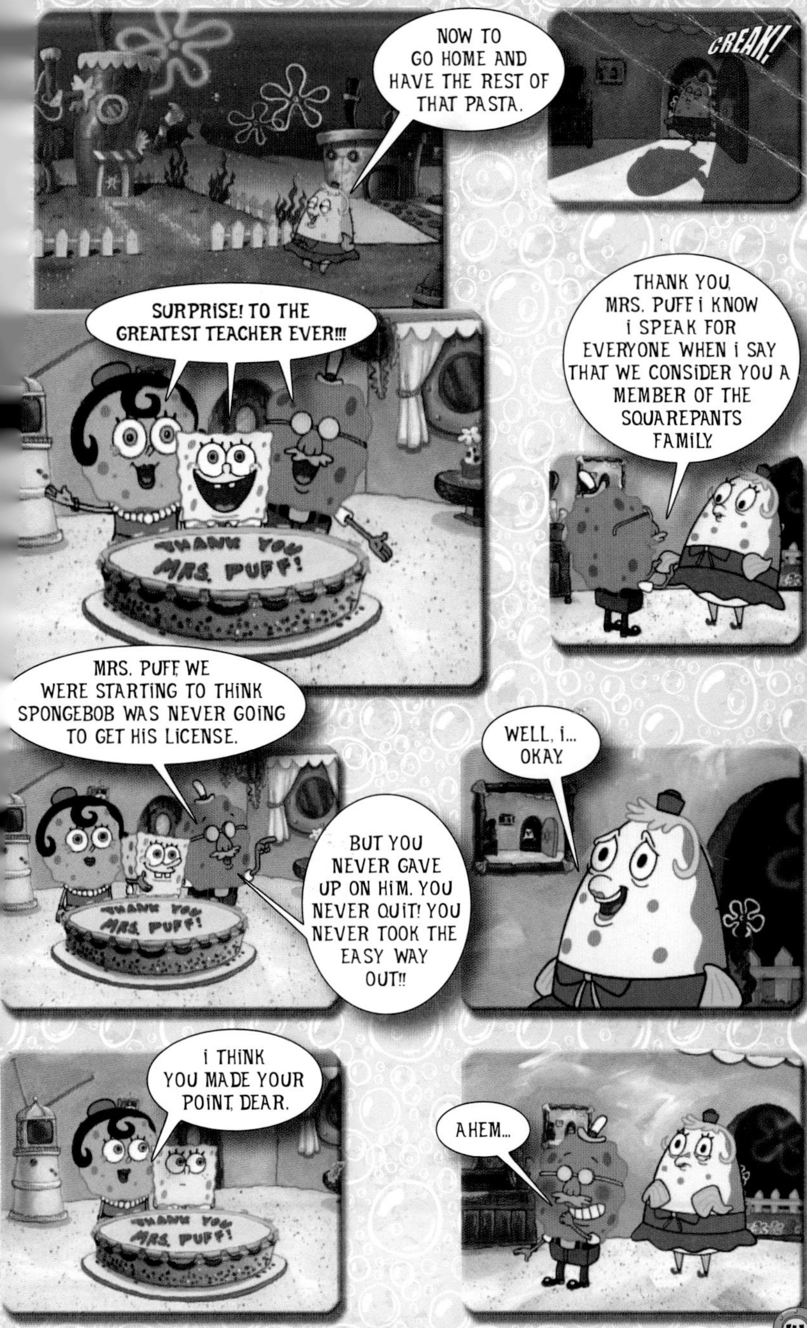

NOW TO GO HOME AND HAVE THE REST OF THAT PASTA.
CREAK!
SURPRISE! TO THE GREATEST TEACHER EVER!!!
THANK YOU MRS. PUFF!
THANK YOU, MRS. PUFF. I KNOW I SPEAK FOR EVERYONE WHEN I SAY THAT WE CONSIDER YOU A MEMBER OF THE SQUAREPANTS FAMILY.
MRS. PUFF, WE WERE STARTING TO THINK SPONGEBOB WAS NEVER GOING TO GET HIS LICENSE.
BUT YOU NEVER GAVE UP ON HIM. YOU NEVER QUIT! YOU NEVER TOOK THE EASY WAY OUT!!
WELL, I... OKAY.
I THINK YOU MADE YOUR POINT, DEAR.
AHEM...

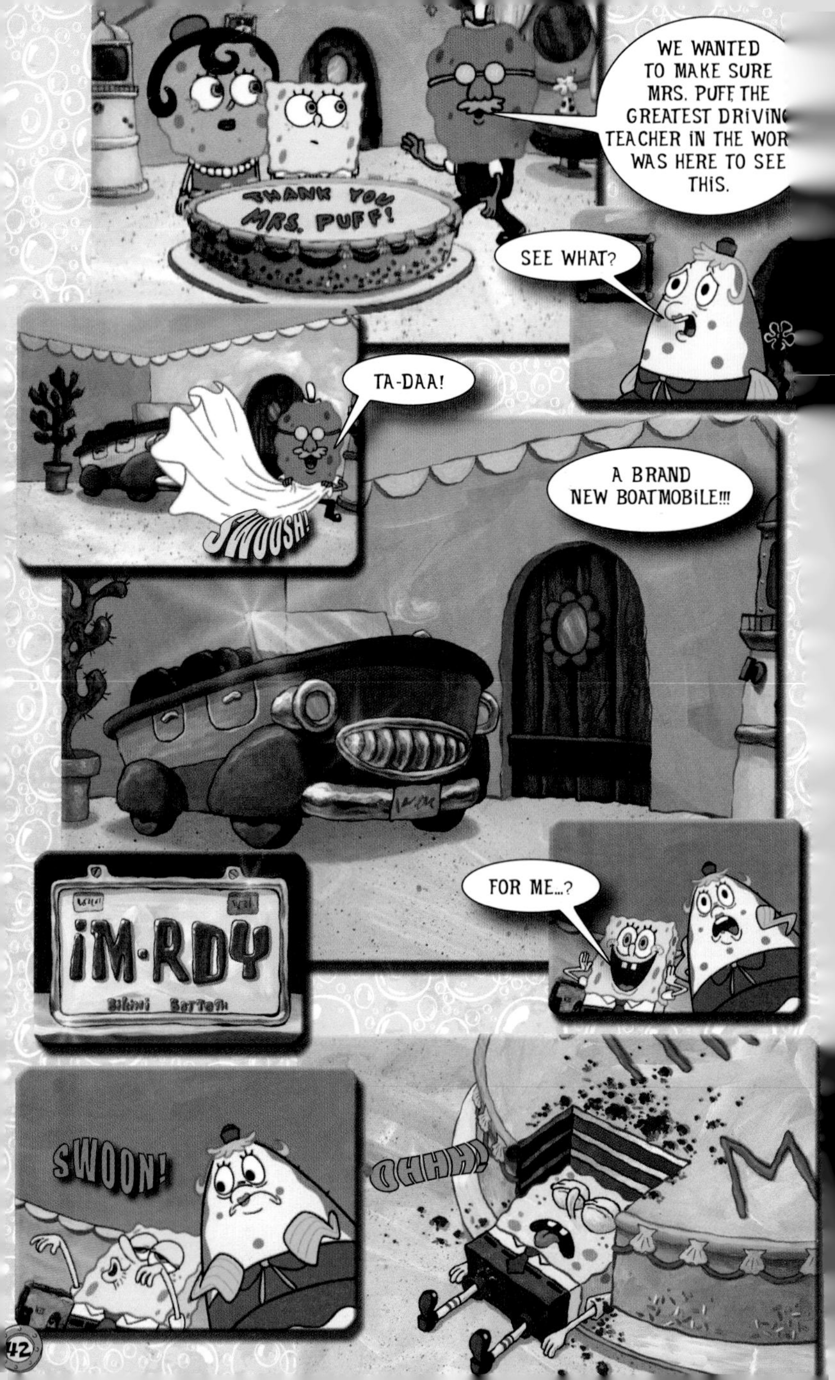
THANK YOU MRS. PUFF!
WE WANTED TO MAKE SURE MRS. PUFF, THE GREATEST DRIVIN TEACHER IN THE WOR WAS HERE TO SEE THIS.
SEE WHAT?
TA-DAA!
SWOOSH!
A BRAND NEW BOATMOBILE!!!
IM-RDY
Bikini Bottom
FOR ME...?
SWOON!
OHHH!

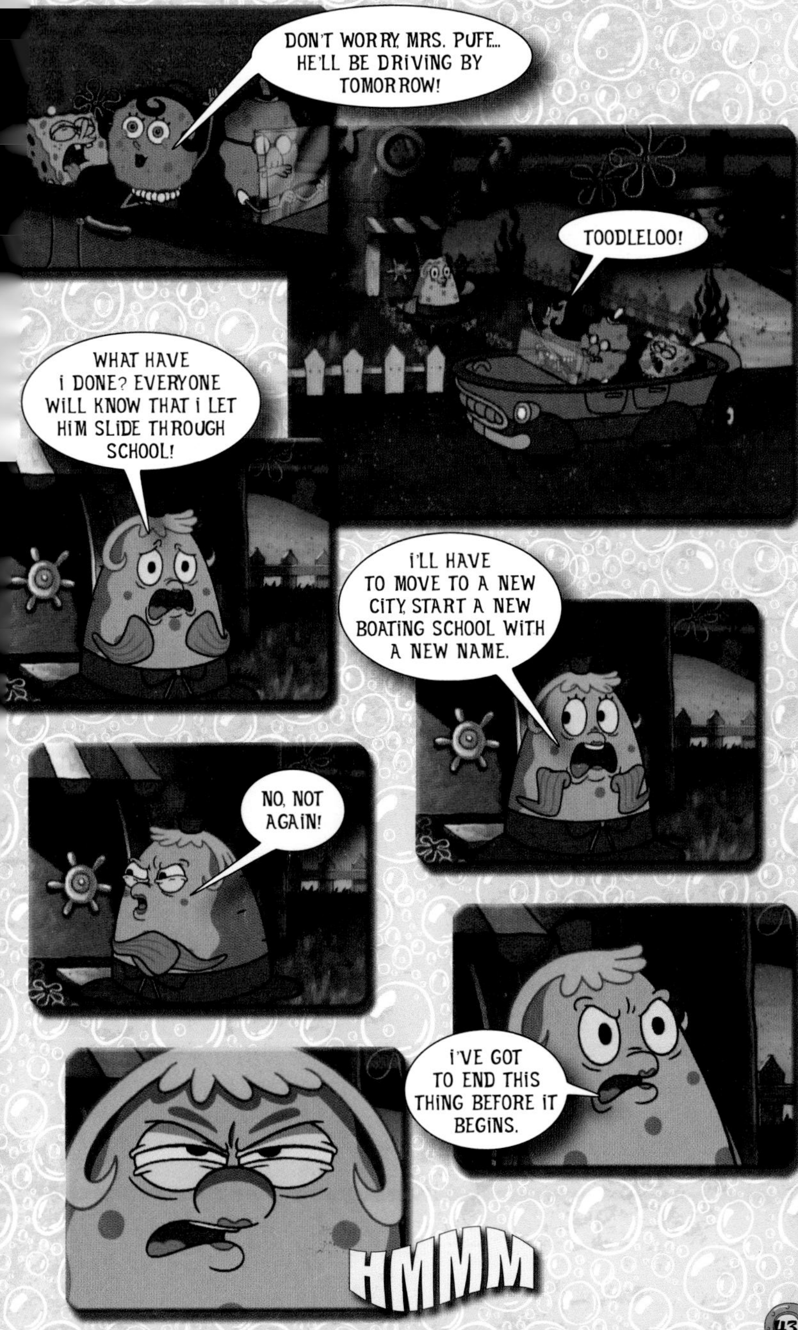
DON'T WORRY, MRS. PUFF... HE'LL BE DRIVING BY TOMORROW!
TOODLELOO!
WHAT HAVE I DONE? EVERYONE WILL KNOW THAT I LET HIM SLIDE THROUGH SCHOOL!
I'LL HAVE TO MOVE TO A NEW CITY, START A NEW BOATING SCHOOL WITH A NEW NAME.
NO, NOT AGAIN!
I'VE GOT TO END THIS THING BEFORE IT BEGINS.
HMMM

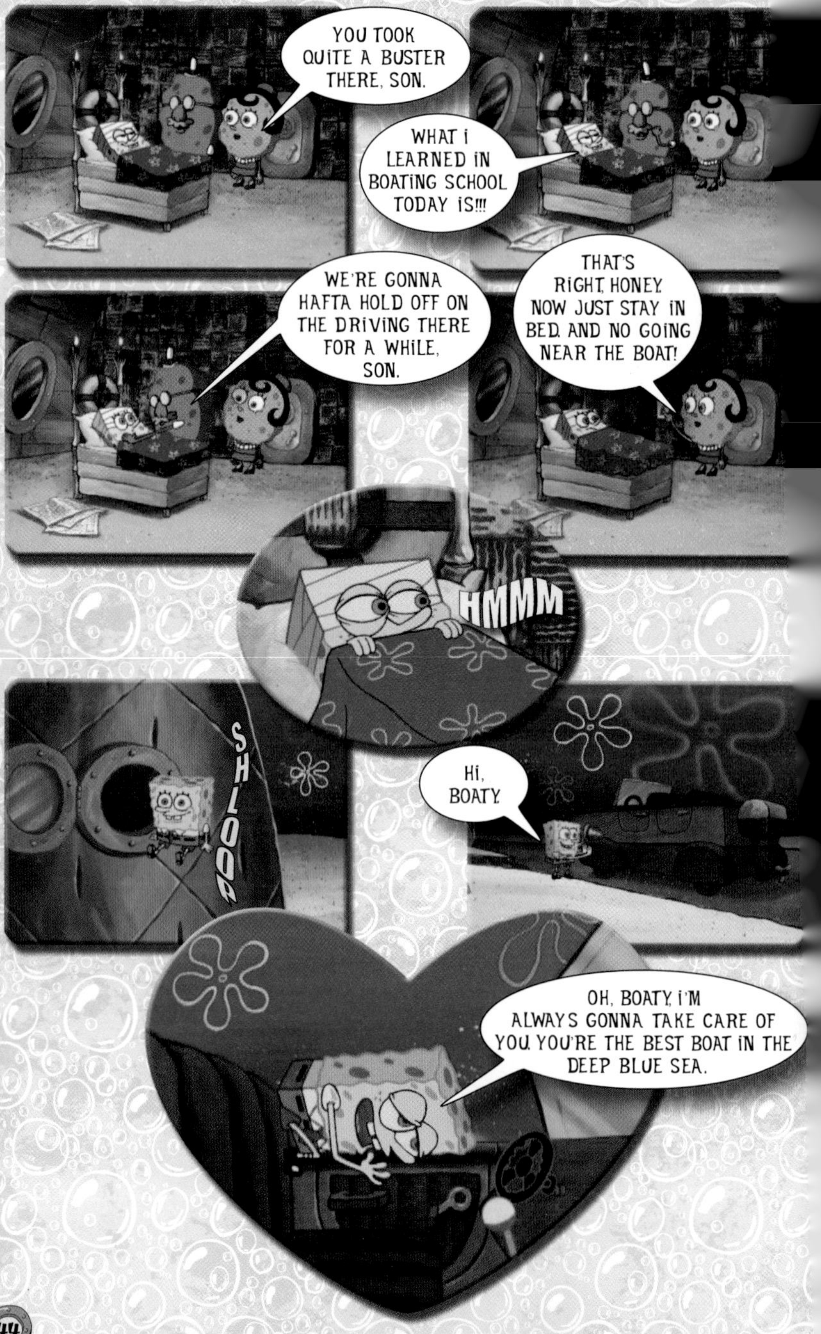
YOU TOOK QUITE A BUSTER THERE, SON.
WHAT I LEARNED IN BOATING SCHOOL TODAY IS!!!
WE'RE GONNA HAFTA HOLD OFF ON THE DRIVING THERE FOR A WHILE, SON.
THAT'S RIGHT, HONEY. NOW JUST STAY IN BED. AND NO GOING NEAR THE BOAT!
HMMM
SHLOOOP
HI, BOATY.
OH, BOATY, I'M ALWAYS GONNA TAKE CARE OF YOU. YOU'RE THE BEST BOAT IN THE DEEP BLUE SEA.

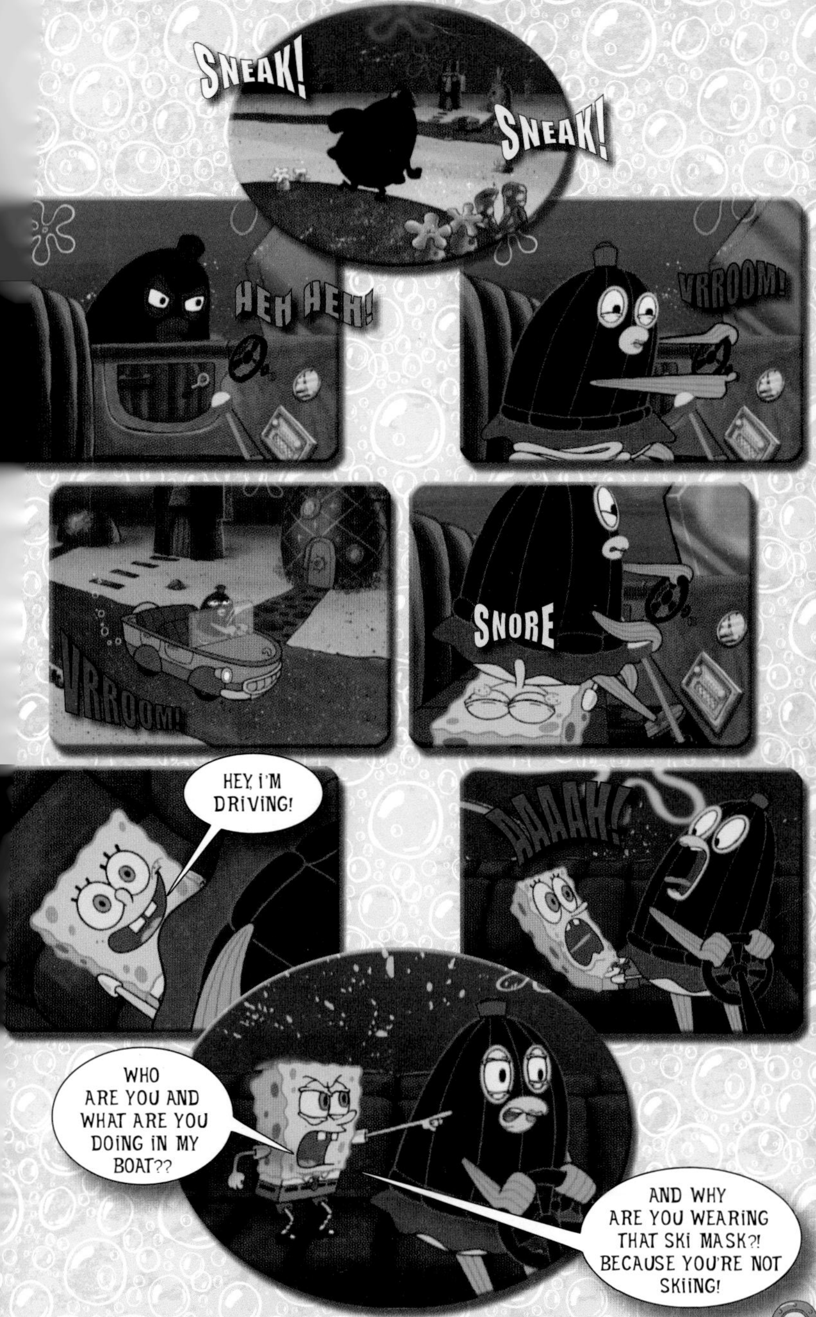
SNEAK!
SNEAK!
HEH HEH!
VRROOM!
VRROOM!
SNORE
HEY, I'M DRIVING!
AAAAH!
WHO ARE YOU AND WHAT ARE YOU DOING IN MY BOAT??
AND WHY ARE YOU WEARING THAT SKI MASK?! BECAUSE YOU'RE NOT SKIING!

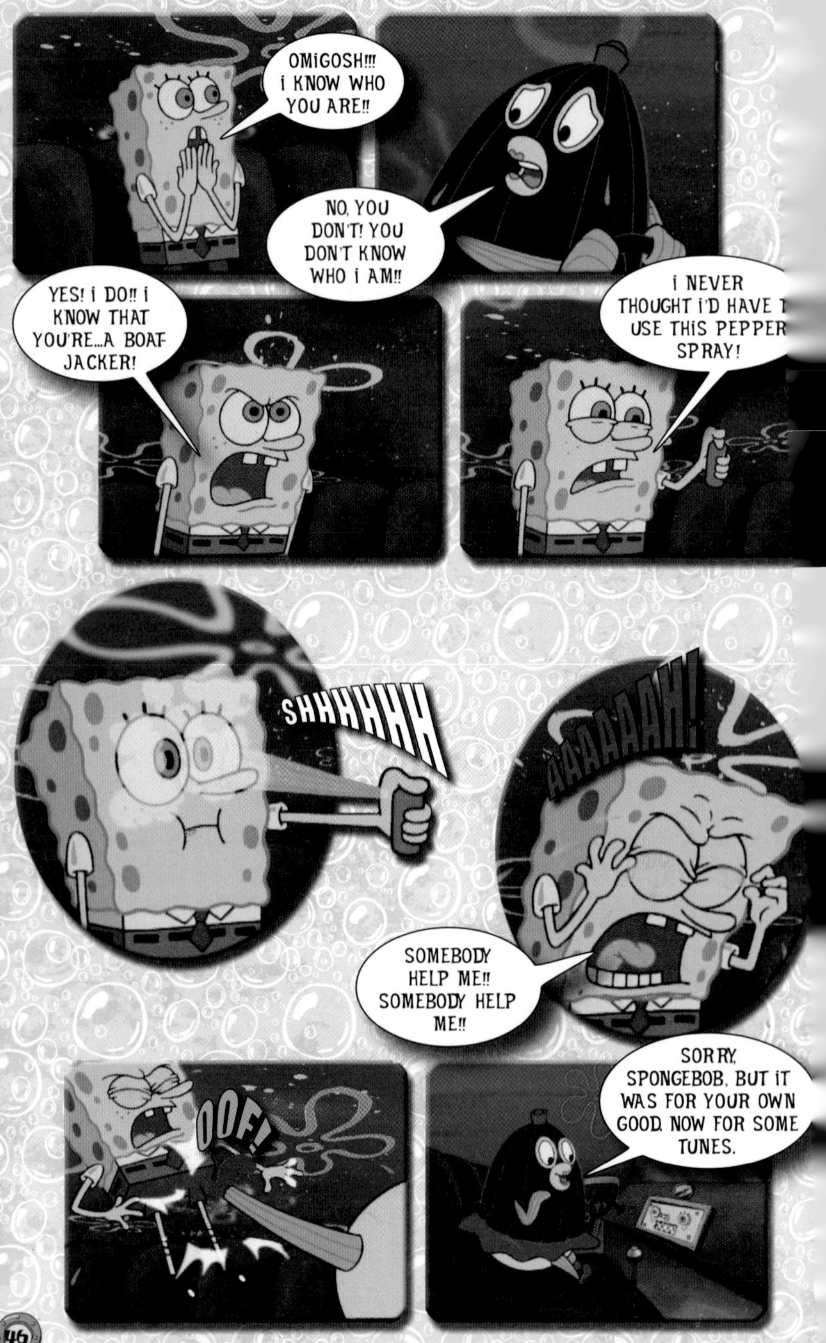
OMiGOSH!!! i KNOW WHO YOU ARE!!
NO, YOU DON'T! YOU DON'T KNOW WHO i AM!!
YES! i DO!! i KNOW THAT YOU'RE...A BOAT-JACKER!
i NEVER THOUGHT i'D HAVE TO USE THiS PEPPER SPRAY!
SHHHHHH
AAAAAAH!
SOMEBODY HELP ME!! SOMEBODY HELP ME!!
OOF!
SORRY, SPONGEBOB, BUT iT WAS FOR YOUR OWN GOOD. NOW FOR SOME TUNES.

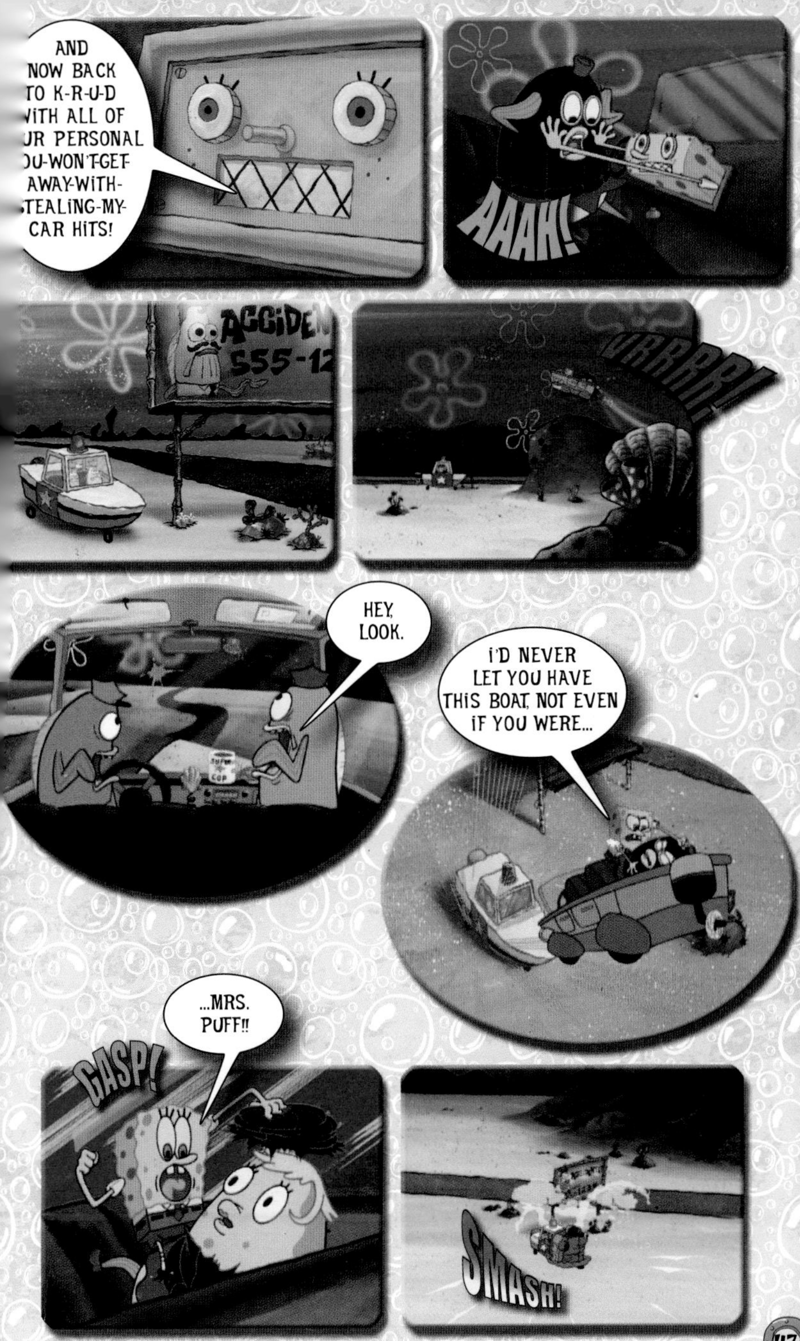
AND NOW BACK TO K-R-U-D VITH ALL OF UR PERSONAL OU-WON'T-GET-AWAY-WITH-TEALING-MY-CAR HITS!
AAAH!
ACCIDEN
555-12
VRRRR!
HEY, LOOK.
I'D NEVER LET YOU HAVE THIS BOAT, NOT EVEN IF YOU WERE...
...MRS. PUFF!!
GASP!
SMASH!

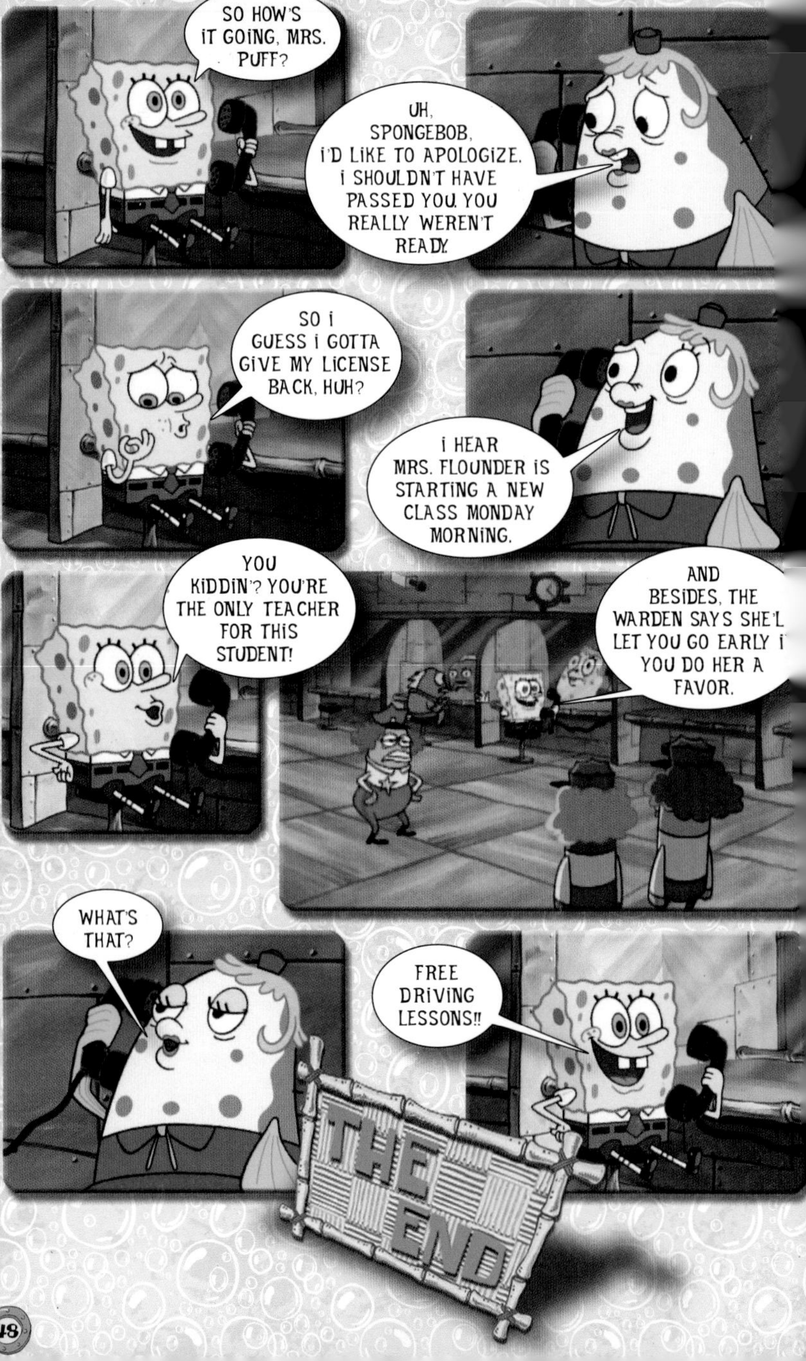
SO HOW'S IT GOING, MRS. PUFF?
UH, SPONGEBOB, I'D LIKE TO APOLOGIZE. I SHOULDN'T HAVE PASSED YOU. YOU REALLY WEREN'T READY.
SO I GUESS I GOTTA GIVE MY LICENSE BACK, HUH?
I HEAR MRS. FLOUNDER IS STARTING A NEW CLASS MONDAY MORNING.
YOU KIDDIN'? YOU'RE THE ONLY TEACHER FOR THIS STUDENT!
AND BESIDES, THE WARDEN SAYS SHE'L LET YOU GO EARLY I YOU DO HER A FAVOR.
WHAT'S THAT?
FREE DRIVING LESSONS!!
THE END

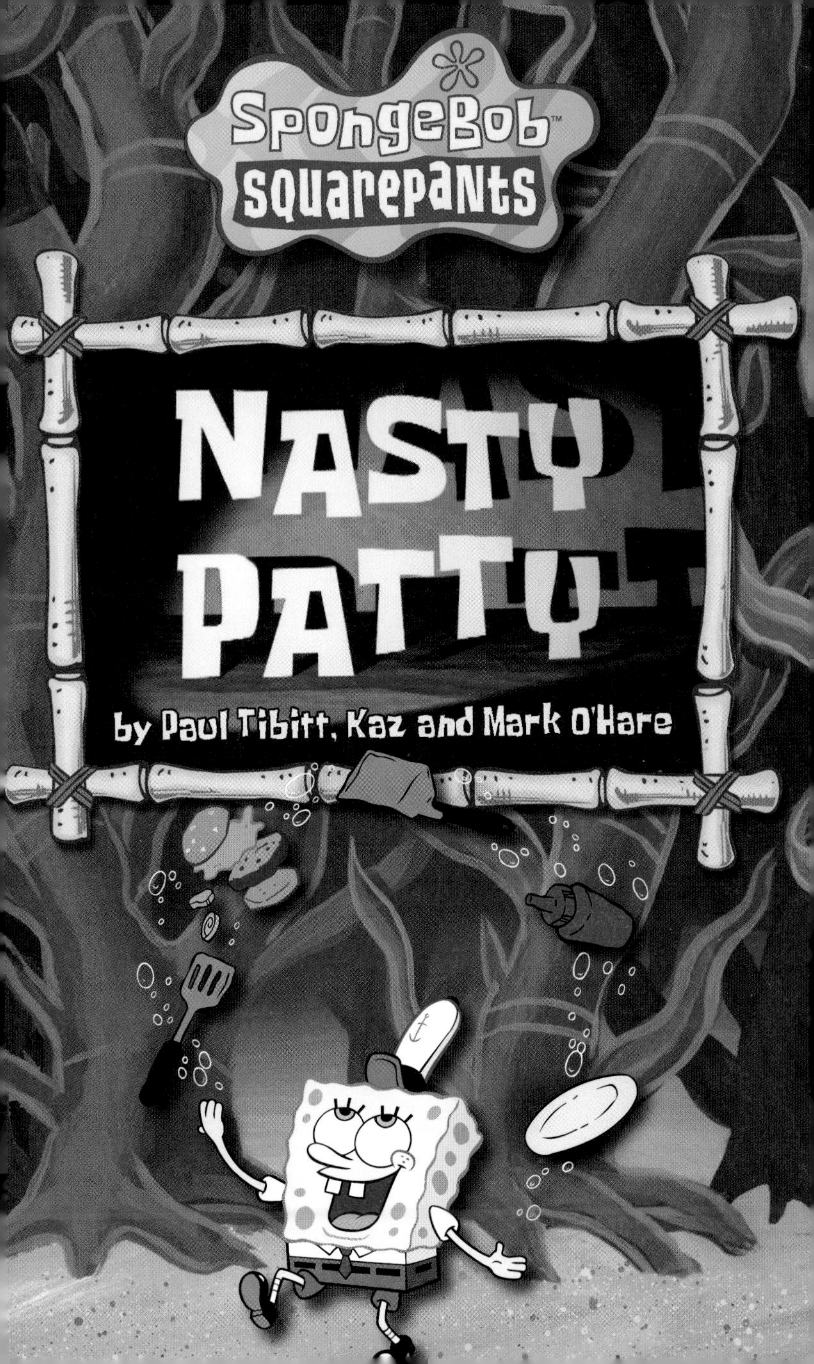
SpongeBob™
SquarePants
NASTY
PATTY
by Paul Tibitt, Kaz and Mark O'Hare

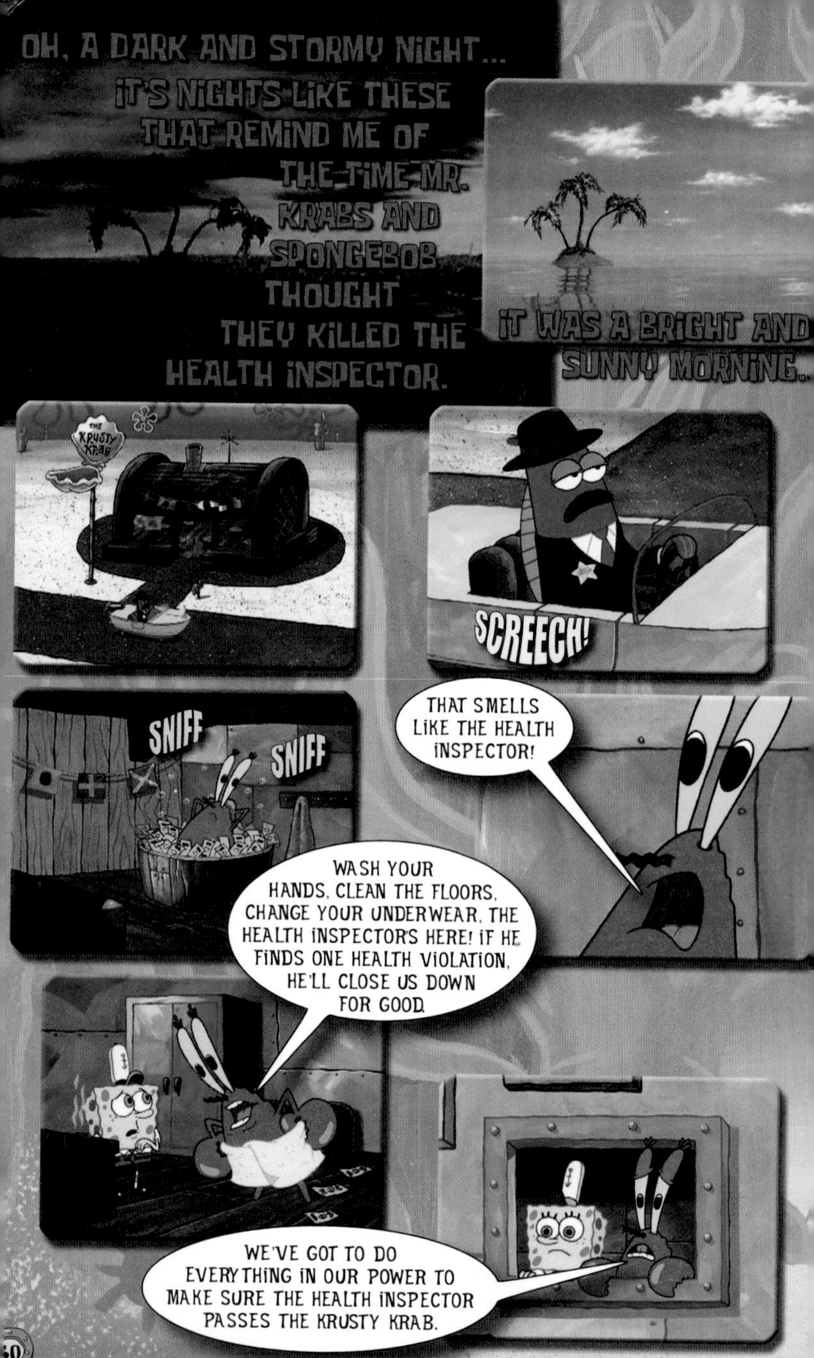
OH, A DARK AND STORMY NIGHT...
IT'S NIGHTS LIKE THESE THAT REMIND ME OF THE TIME MR. KRABS AND SPONGEBOB THOUGHT THEY KILLED THE HEALTH INSPECTOR.
IT WAS A BRIGHT AND SUNNY MORNING...
THE KRUSTY KRAB
SCREECH!
SNIFF
SNIFF
THAT SMELLS LIKE THE HEALTH INSPECTOR!
WASH YOUR HANDS, CLEAN THE FLOORS, CHANGE YOUR UNDERWEAR, THE HEALTH INSPECTOR'S HERE! IF HE FINDS ONE HEALTH VIOLATION, HE'LL CLOSE US DOWN FOR GOOD.
WE'VE GOT TO DO EVERYTHING IN OUR POWER TO MAKE SURE THE HEALTH INSPECTOR PASSES THE KRUSTY KRAB.

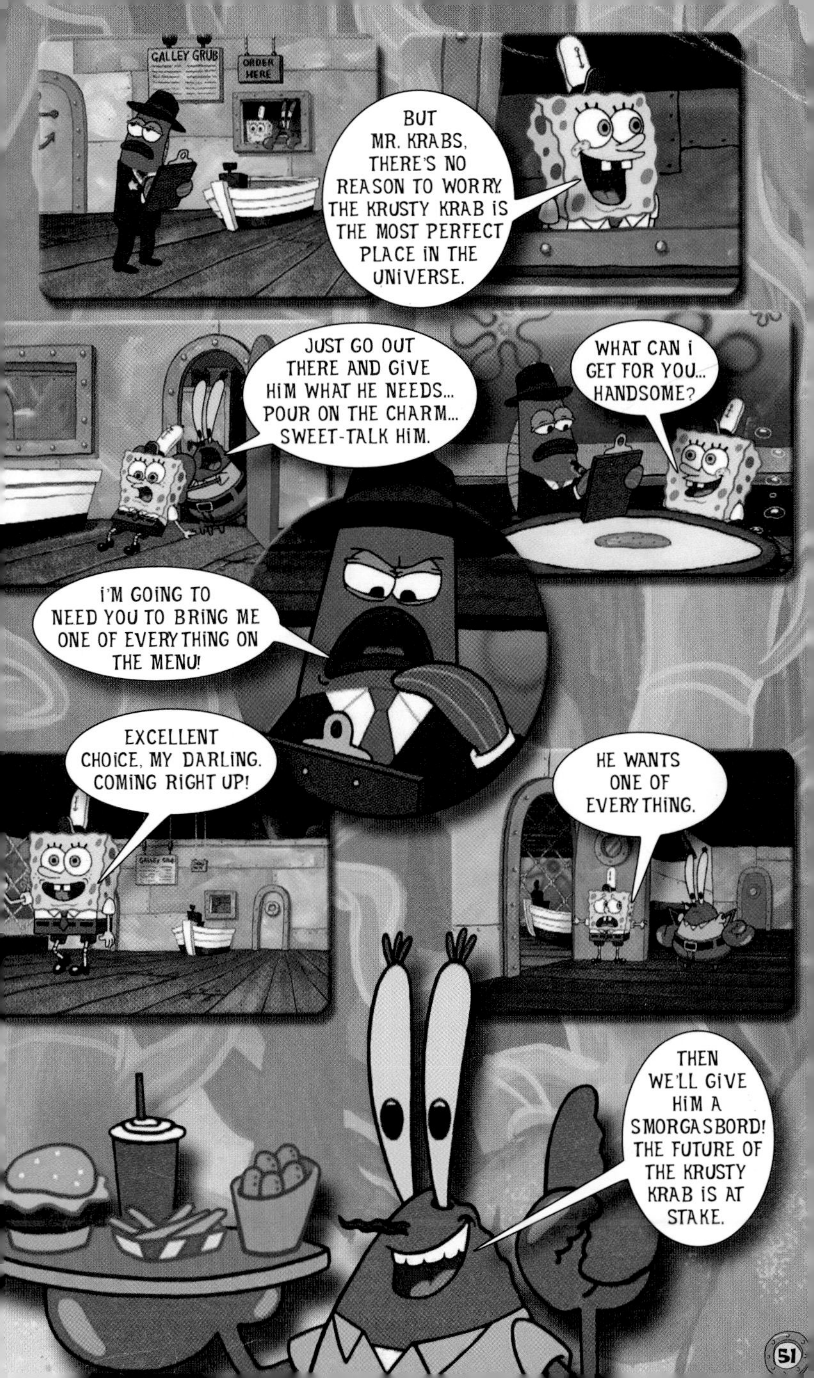
GALLEY GRUB
ORDER HERE
BUT MR. KRABS, THERE'S NO REASON TO WORRY. THE KRUSTY KRAB IS THE MOST PERFECT PLACE IN THE UNIVERSE.
JUST GO OUT THERE AND GIVE HIM WHAT HE NEEDS... POUR ON THE CHARM... SWEET-TALK HIM.
WHAT CAN I GET FOR YOU... HANDSOME?
I'M GOING TO NEED YOU TO BRING ME ONE OF EVERYTHING ON THE MENU!
EXCELLENT CHOICE, MY DARLING. COMING RIGHT UP!
HE WANTS ONE OF EVERYTHING.
THEN WE'LL GIVE HIM A SMORGASBORD! THE FUTURE OF THE KRUSTY KRAB IS AT STAKE.

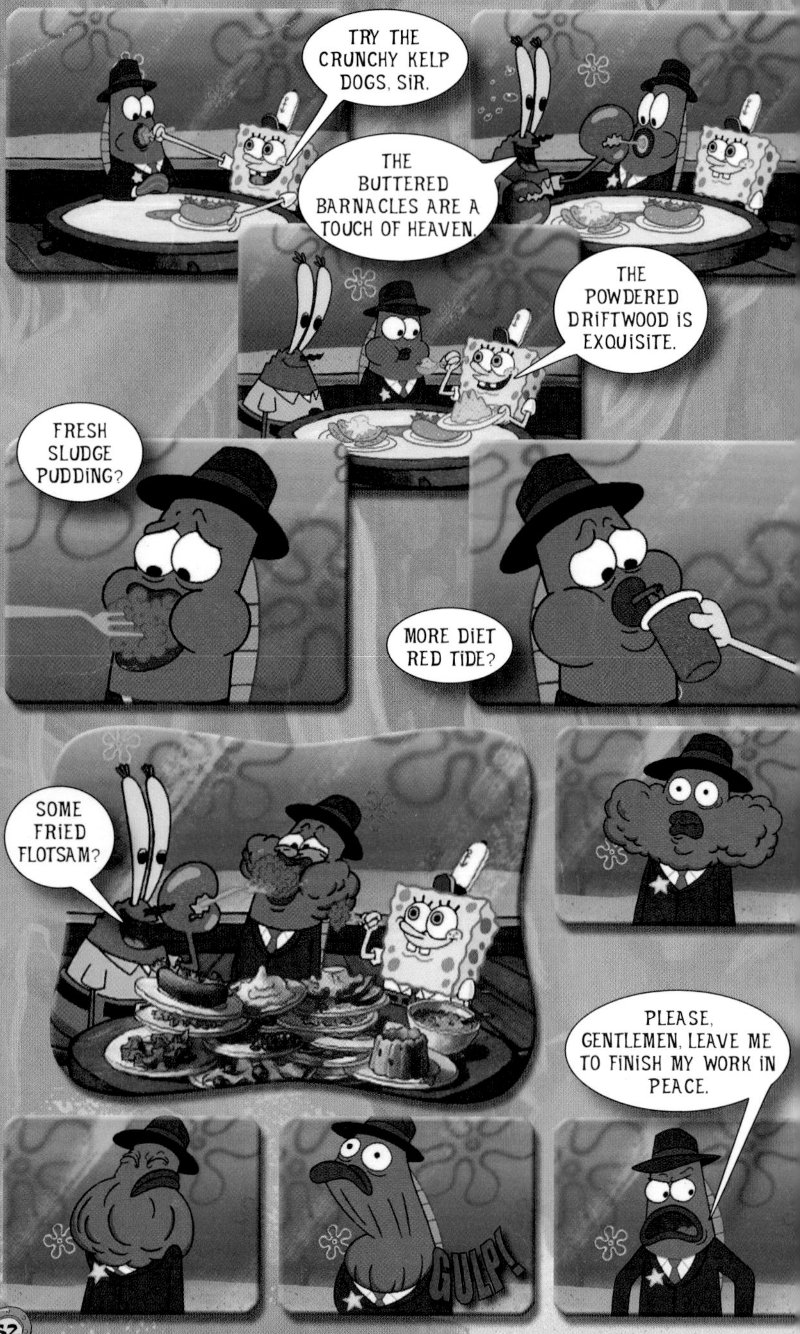
TRY THE CRUNCHY KELP DOGS, SIR.
THE BUTTERED BARNACLES ARE A TOUCH OF HEAVEN.
THE POWDERED DRIFTWOOD IS EXQUISITE.
FRESH SLUDGE PUDDING?
MORE DIET RED TIDE?
SOME FRIED FLOTSAM?
PLEASE, GENTLEMEN, LEAVE ME TO FINISH MY WORK IN PEACE.
GULP!

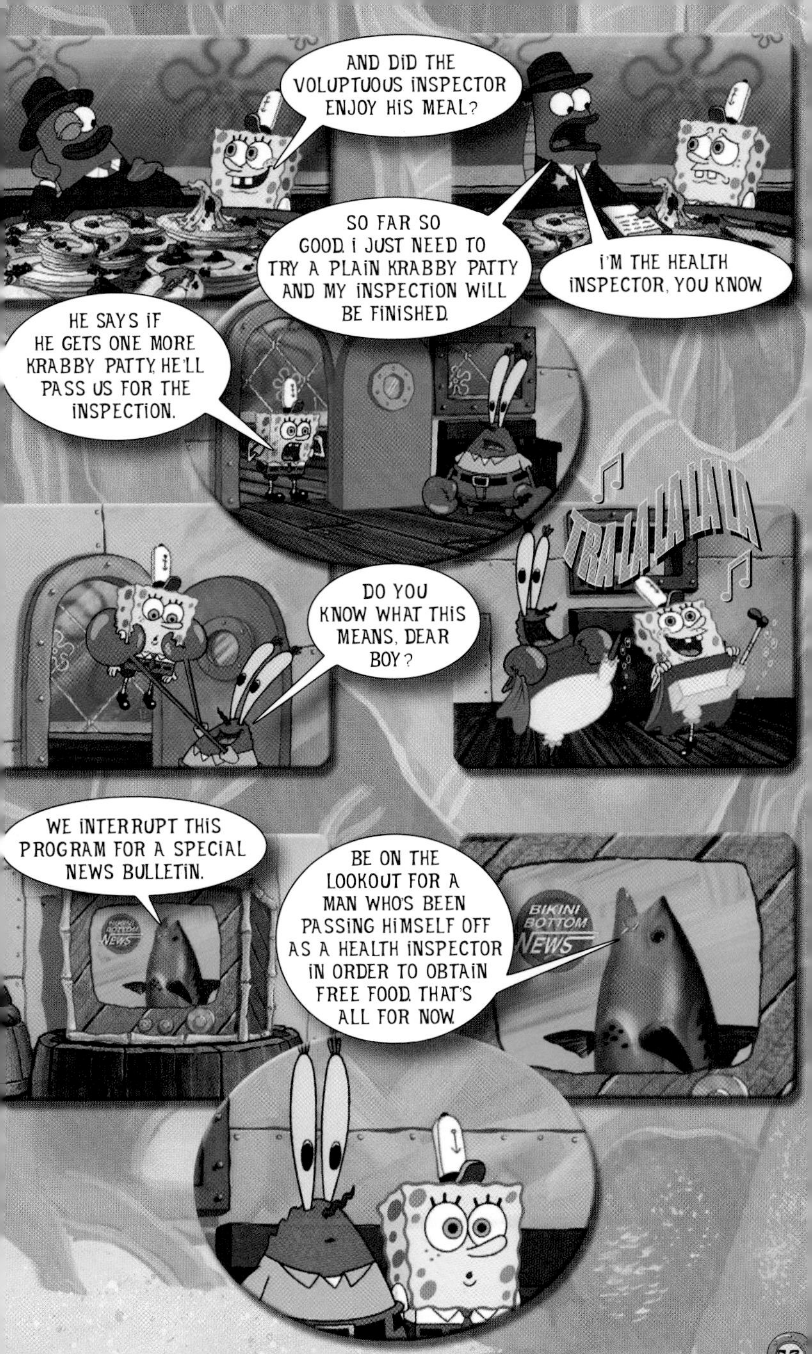

AND DID THE VOLUPTUOUS INSPECTOR ENJOY HIS MEAL?
SO FAR SO GOOD. I JUST NEED TO TRY A PLAIN KRABBY PATTY AND MY INSPECTION WILL BE FINISHED.
I'M THE HEALTH INSPECTOR, YOU KNOW.
HE SAYS IF HE GETS ONE MORE KRABBY PATTY, HE'LL PASS US FOR THE INSPECTION.
DO YOU KNOW WHAT THIS MEANS, DEAR BOY?
TRA LA LA LA LA
WE INTERRUPT THIS PROGRAM FOR A SPECIAL NEWS BULLETIN.
BE ON THE LOOKOUT FOR A MAN WHO'S BEEN PASSING HIMSELF OFF AS A HEALTH INSPECTOR IN ORDER TO OBTAIN FREE FOOD. THAT'S ALL FOR NOW.
BIKINI BOTTOM NEWS

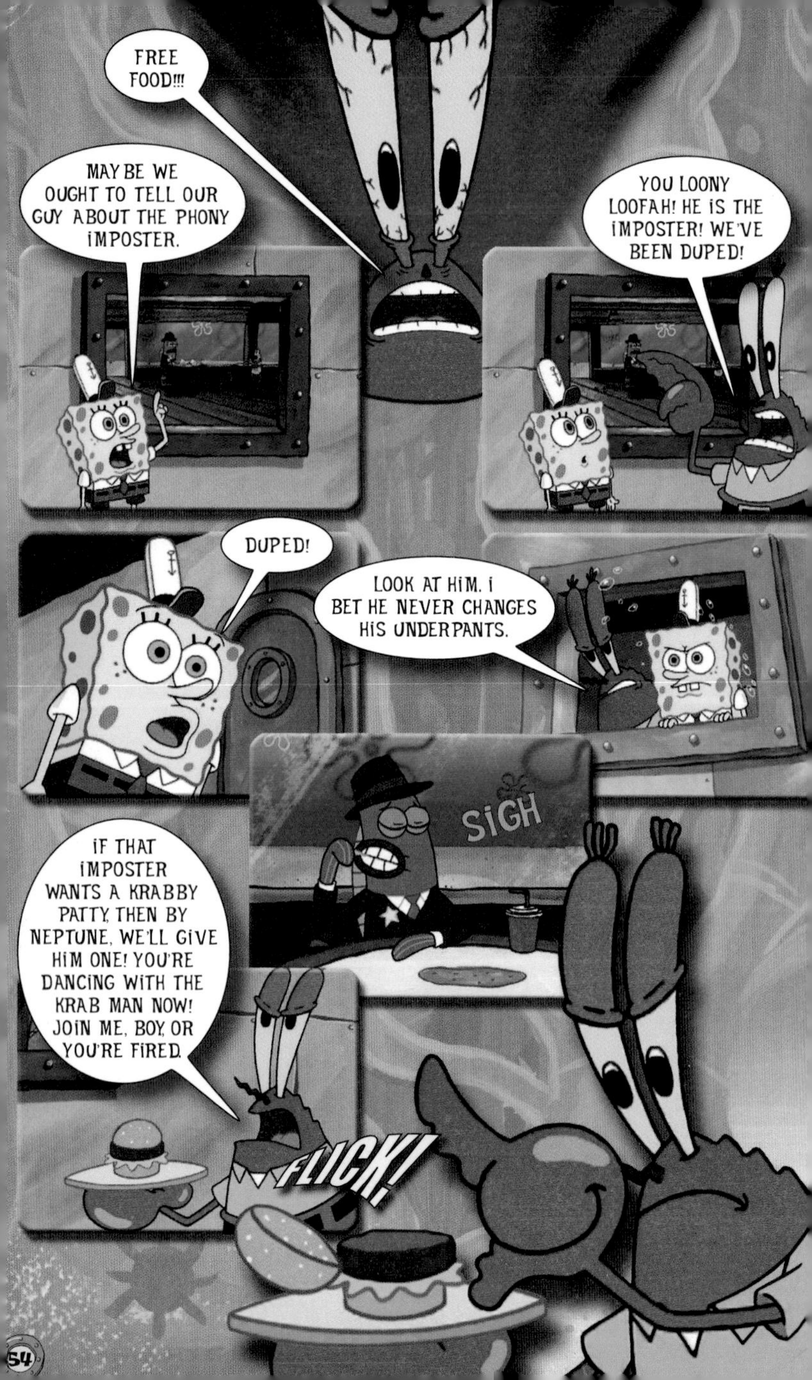

FREE FOOD!!!
MAYBE WE OUGHT TO TELL OUR GUY ABOUT THE PHONY IMPOSTER.
YOU LOONY LOOFAH! HE IS THE IMPOSTER! WE'VE BEEN DUPED!
DUPED!
LOOK AT HIM. I BET HE NEVER CHANGES HIS UNDERPANTS.
SIGH
IF THAT IMPOSTER WANTS A KRABBY PATTY, THEN BY NEPTUNE, WE'LL GIVE HIM ONE! YOU'RE DANCING WITH THE KRAB MAN NOW! JOIN ME, BOY, OR YOU'RE FIRED.
FLICK!

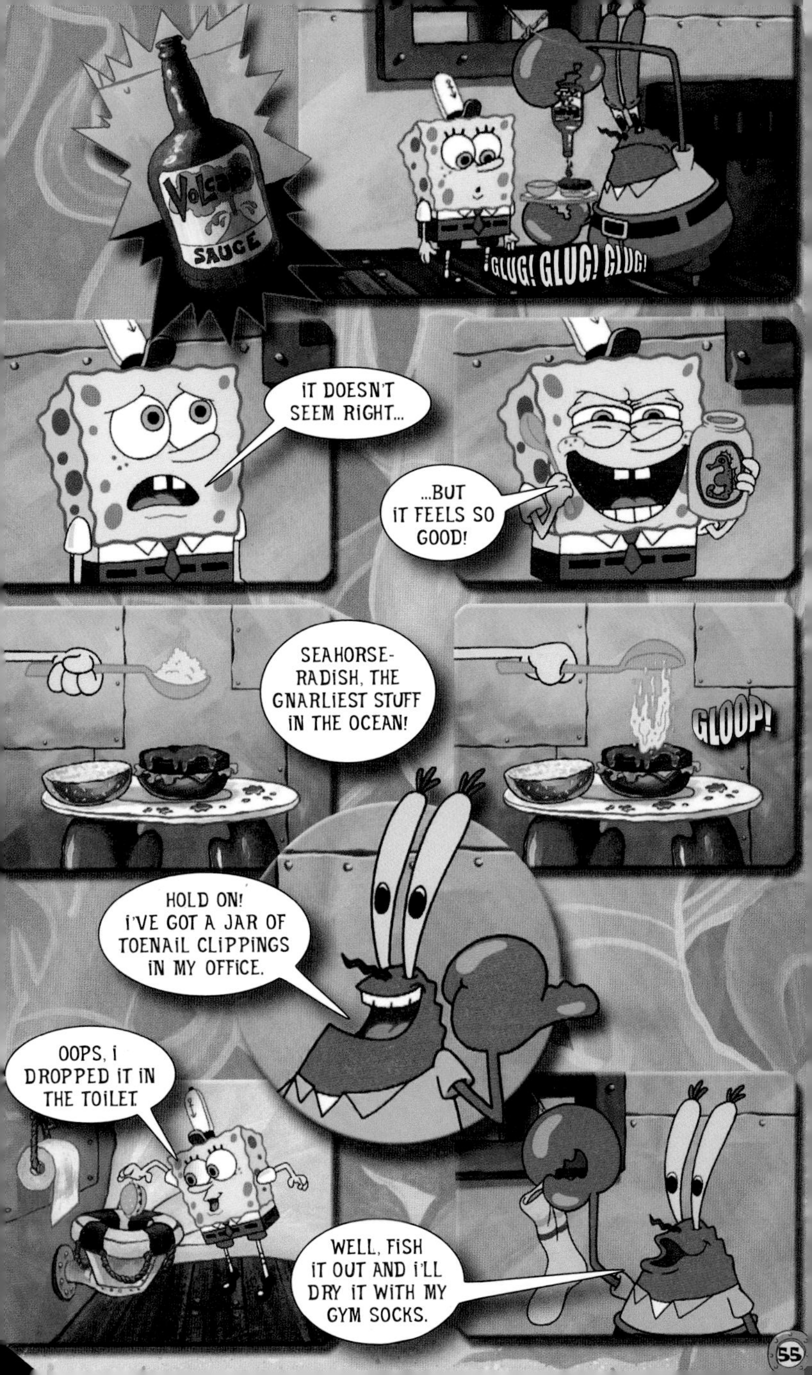

VoLcano
SAUCE
GLUG! GLUG! GLUG!
IT DOESN'T SEEM RIGHT...
...BUT IT FEELS SO GOOD!
SEAHORSE-RADISH, THE GNARLIEST STUFF IN THE OCEAN!
GLOOP!
HOLD ON! I'VE GOT A JAR OF TOENAIL CLIPPINGS IN MY OFFICE.
OOPS, I DROPPED IT IN THE TOILET.
WELL, FISH IT OUT AND I'LL DRY IT WITH MY GYM SOCKS.

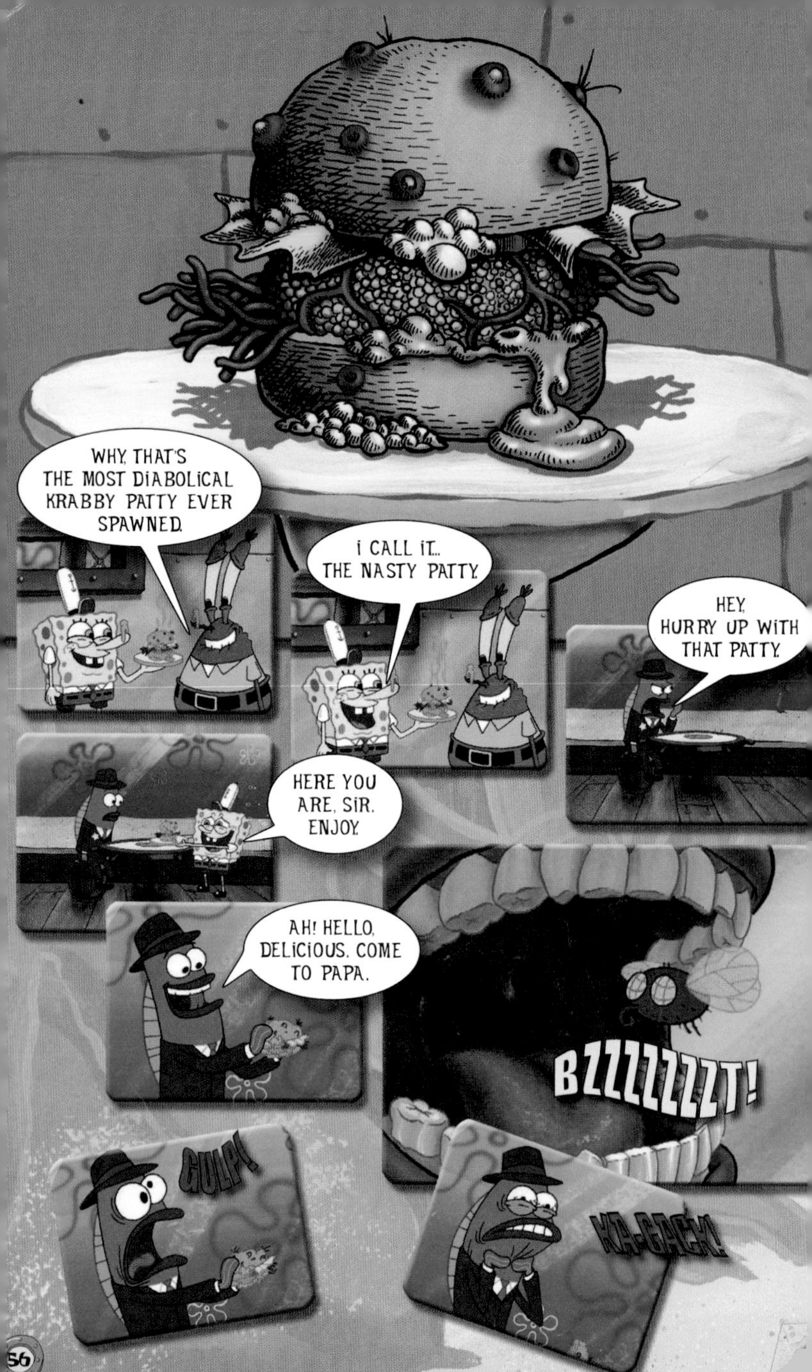

WHY, THAT'S THE MOST DIABOLICAL KRABBY PATTY EVER SPAWNED.
I CALL IT... THE NASTY PATTY.
HEY, HURRY UP WITH THAT PATTY.
HERE YOU ARE, SIR. ENJOY.
AH! HELLO, DELICIOUS. COME TO PAPA.
BZZZZZZZT!
GULP!
KA-GACK!

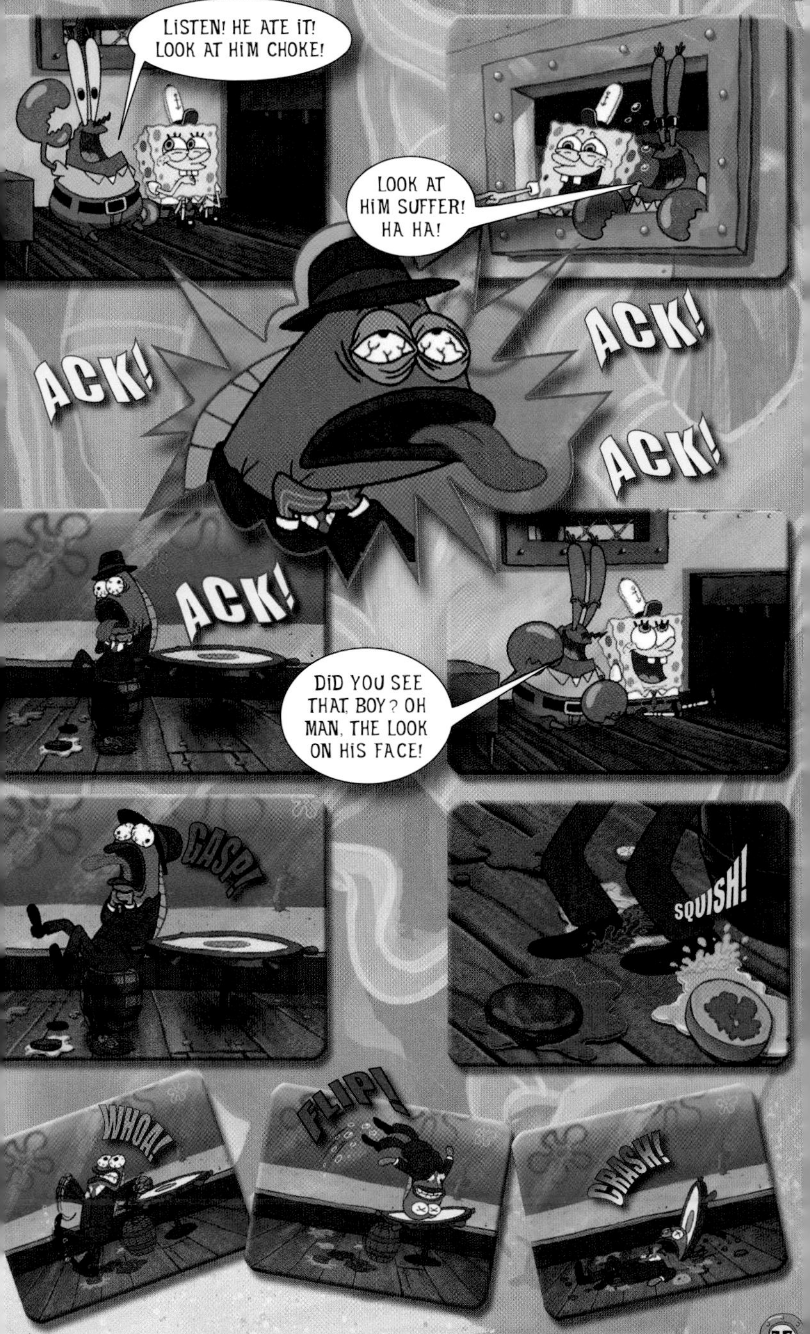
LISTEN! HE ATE IT! LOOK AT HIM CHOKE!
LOOK AT HIM SUFFER! HA HA!
ACK!
ACK!
ACK!
ACK!
DID YOU SEE THAT, BOY? OH MAN, THE LOOK ON HIS FACE!
GASP!
SQUISH!
WHOA!
FLIP!
CRASH!

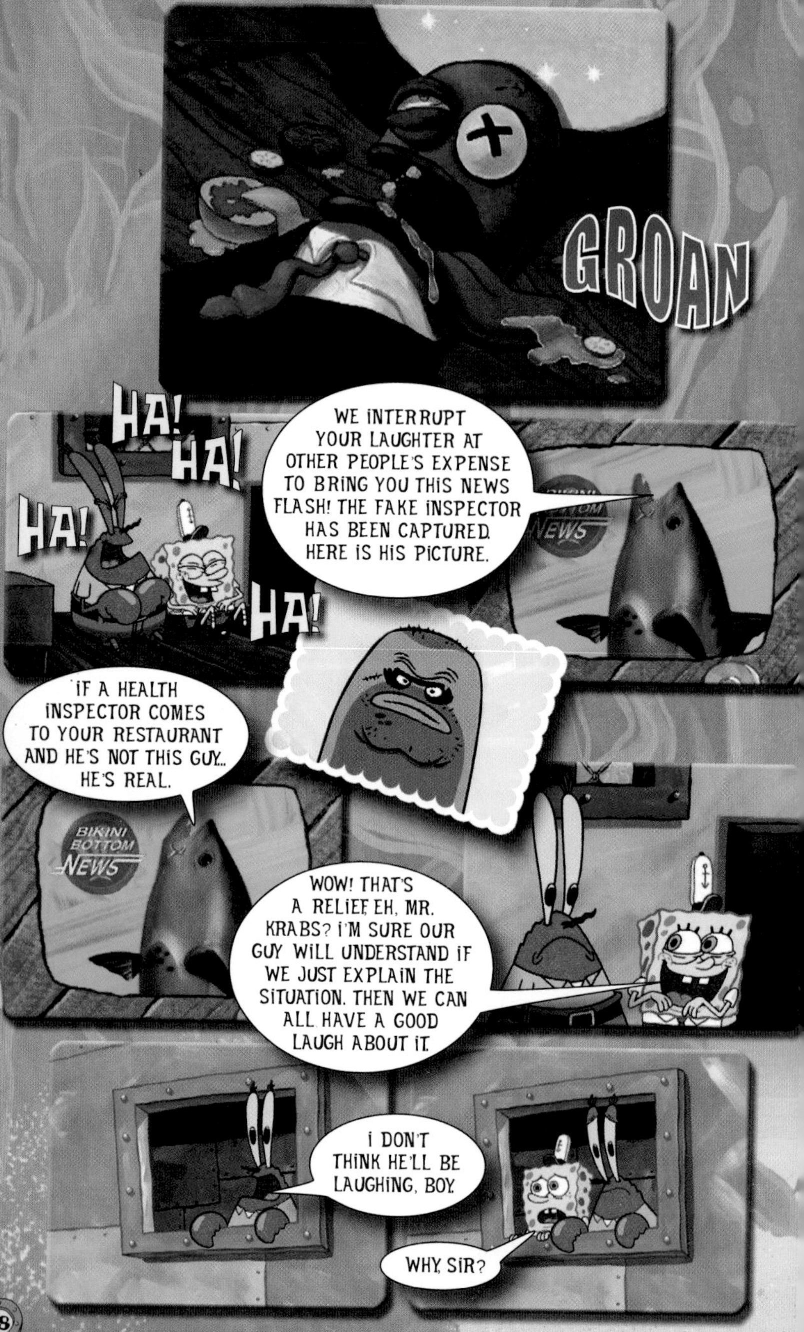
GROAN
HA! HA! HA! HA!
WE INTERRUPT YOUR LAUGHTER AT OTHER PEOPLE'S EXPENSE TO BRING YOU THIS NEWS FLASH! THE FAKE INSPECTOR HAS BEEN CAPTURED. HERE IS HIS PICTURE.
IF A HEALTH INSPECTOR COMES TO YOUR RESTAURANT AND HE'S NOT THIS GUY... HE'S REAL.
BIKINI BOTTOM NEWS
WOW! THAT'S A RELIEF, EH, MR. KRABS? I'M SURE OUR GUY WILL UNDERSTAND IF WE JUST EXPLAIN THE SITUATION. THEN WE CAN ALL HAVE A GOOD LAUGH ABOUT IT.
I DON'T THINK HE'LL BE LAUGHING, BOY.
WHY, SIR?

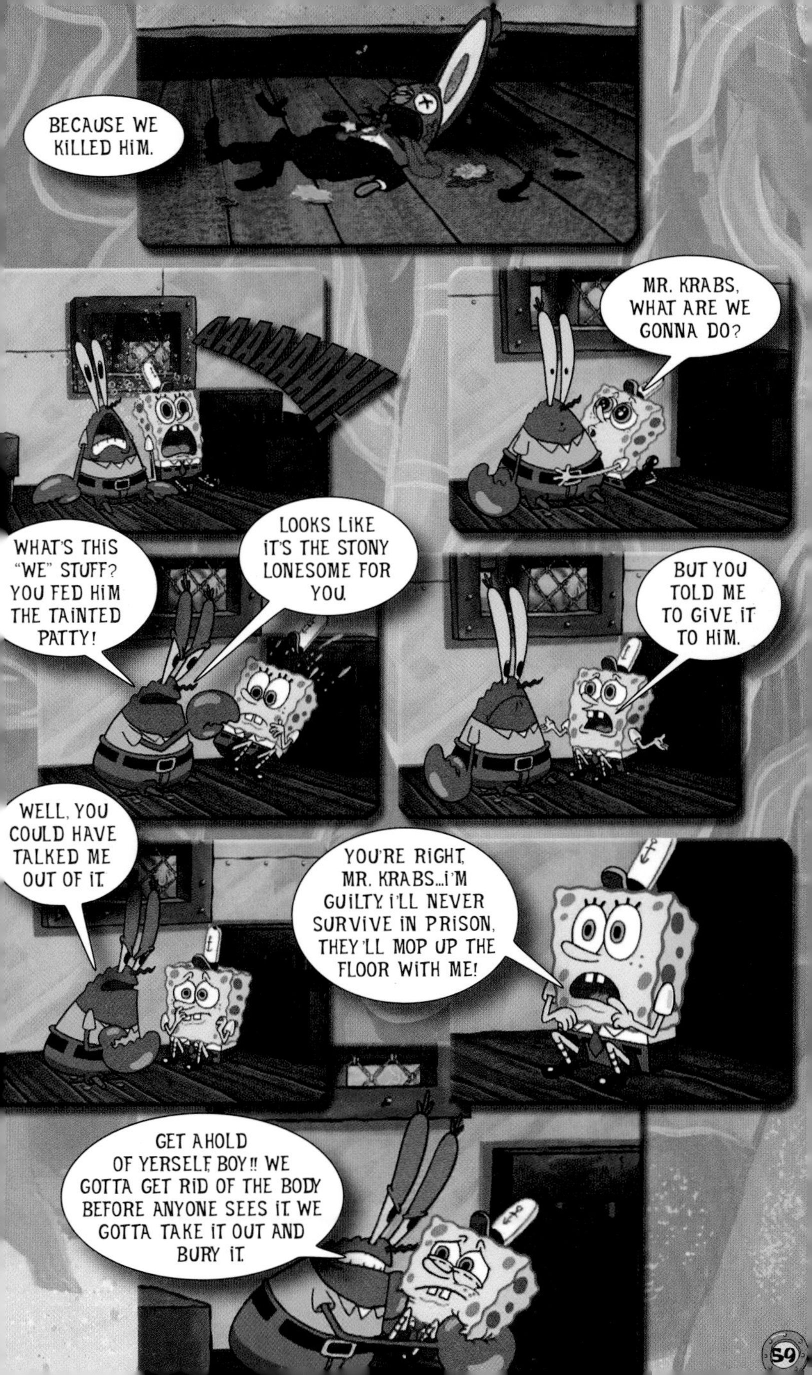
BECAUSE WE KILLED HIM.
AAAAAAAHHH!
MR. KRABS, WHAT ARE WE GONNA DO?
WHAT'S THIS "WE" STUFF? YOU FED HIM THE TAINTED PATTY!
LOOKS LIKE IT'S THE STONY LONESOME FOR YOU.
BUT YOU TOLD ME TO GIVE IT TO HIM.
WELL, YOU COULD HAVE TALKED ME OUT OF IT.
YOU'RE RIGHT, MR. KRABS...I'M GUILTY. I'LL NEVER SURVIVE IN PRISON, THEY'LL MOP UP THE FLOOR WITH ME!
GET AHOLD OF YERSELF, BOY!! WE GOTTA GET RID OF THE BODY BEFORE ANYONE SEES IT. WE GOTTA TAKE IT OUT AND BURY IT.

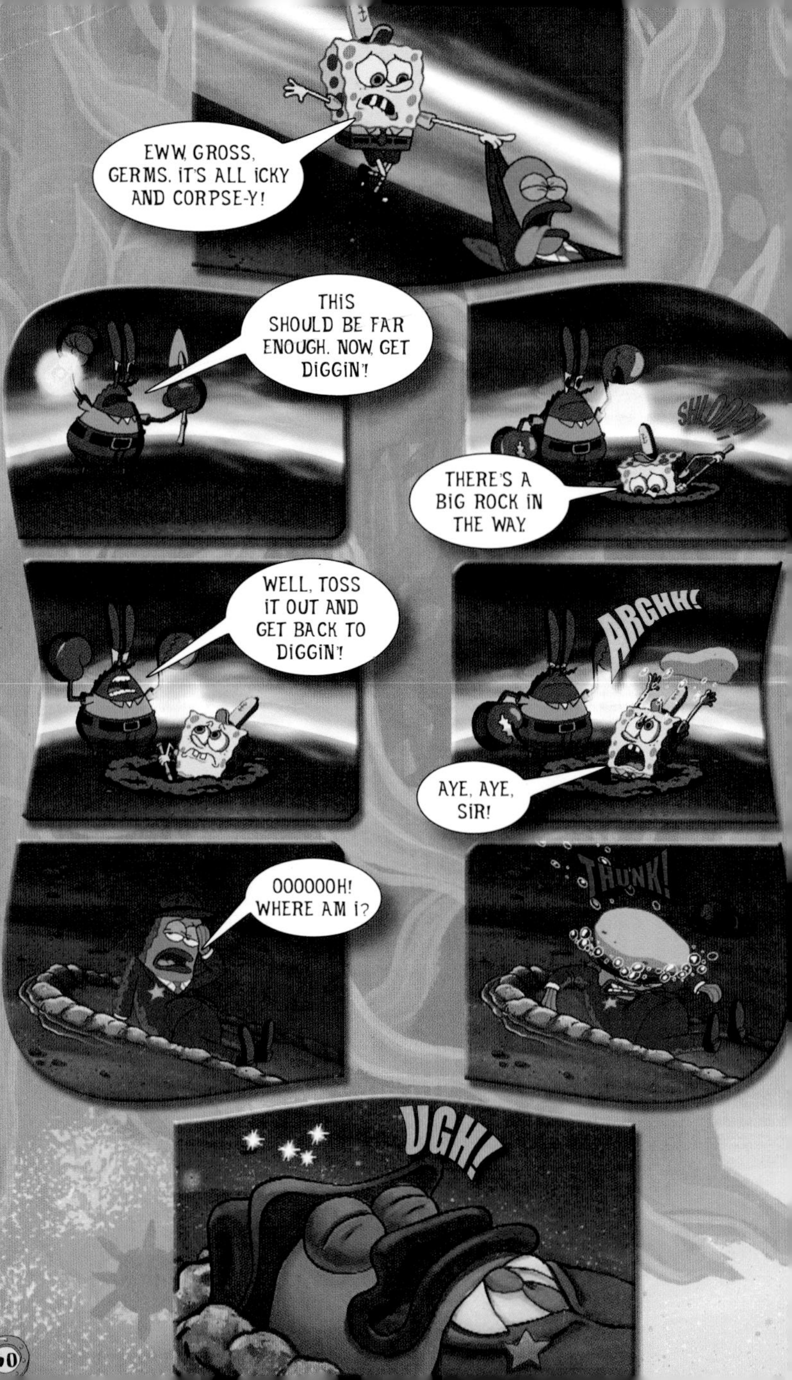
EWW, GROSS, GERMS. IT'S ALL ICKY AND CORPSE-Y!
THIS SHOULD BE FAR ENOUGH. NOW, GET DIGGIN'!
THERE'S A BIG ROCK IN THE WAY.
WELL, TOSS IT OUT AND GET BACK TO DIGGIN'!
ARGHH!
AYE, AYE, SIR!
OOOOOOH! WHERE AM I?
THUNK!
UGH!

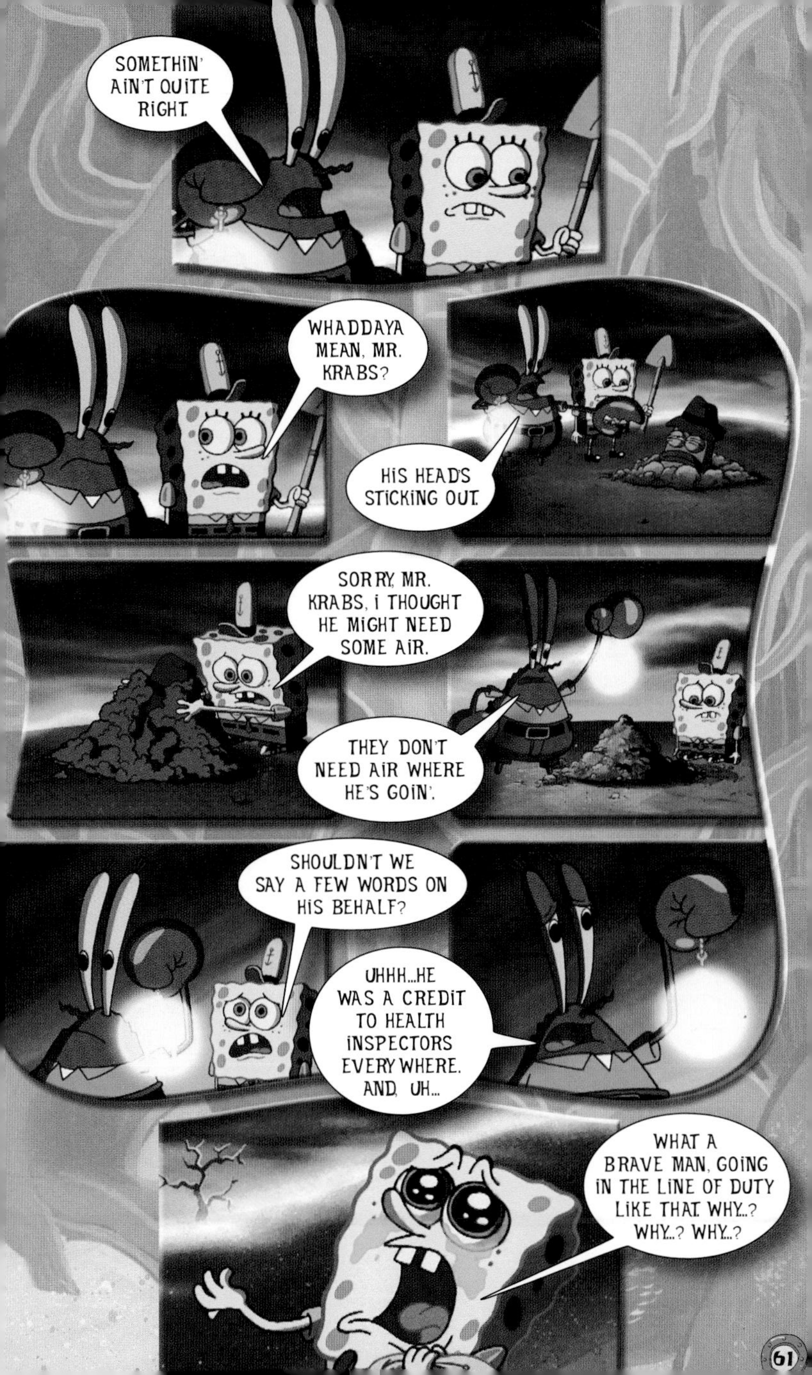
SOMETHIN' AIN'T QUITE RIGHT.
WHADDAYA MEAN, MR. KRABS?
HIS HEAD'S STICKING OUT.
SORRY, MR. KRABS, I THOUGHT HE MIGHT NEED SOME AIR.
THEY DON'T NEED AIR WHERE HE'S GOIN'.
SHOULDN'T WE SAY A FEW WORDS ON HIS BEHALF?
UHHH...HE WAS A CREDIT TO HEALTH INSPECTORS EVERYWHERE. AND, UH...
WHAT A BRAVE MAN, GOING IN THE LINE OF DUTY LIKE THAT. WHY...? WHY...? WHY...?

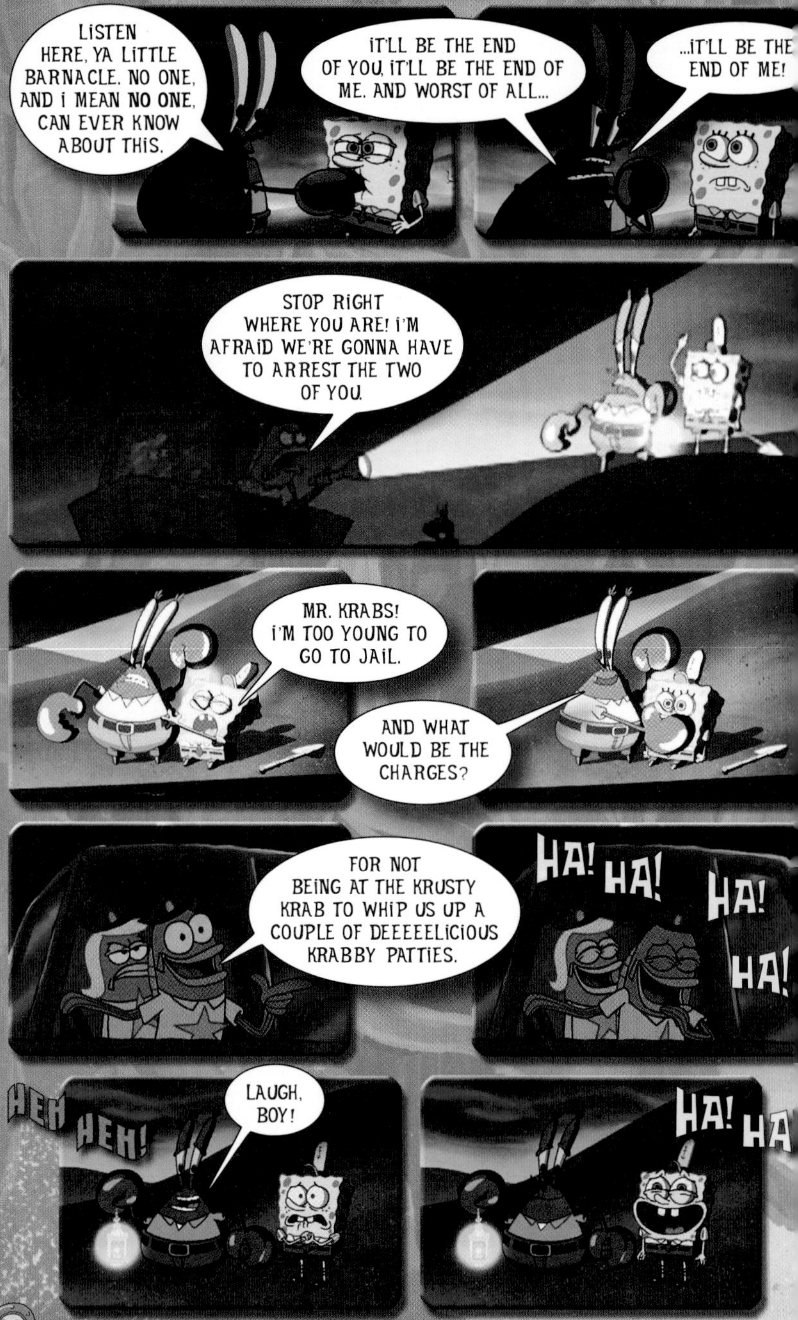
LISTEN HERE, YA LITTLE BARNACLE. NO ONE, AND I MEAN NO ONE, CAN EVER KNOW ABOUT THIS.
IT'LL BE THE END OF YOU, IT'LL BE THE END OF ME. AND WORST OF ALL...
...IT'LL BE THE END OF ME!
STOP RIGHT WHERE YOU ARE! I'M AFRAID WE'RE GONNA HAVE TO ARREST THE TWO OF YOU.
MR. KRABS! I'M TOO YOUNG TO GO TO JAIL.
AND WHAT WOULD BE THE CHARGES?
FOR NOT BEING AT THE KRUSTY KRAB TO WHIP US UP A COUPLE OF DEEEEELICIOUS KRABBY PATTIES.
HA! HA! HA! HA!
HEH HEH!
LAUGH, BOY!
HA! HA

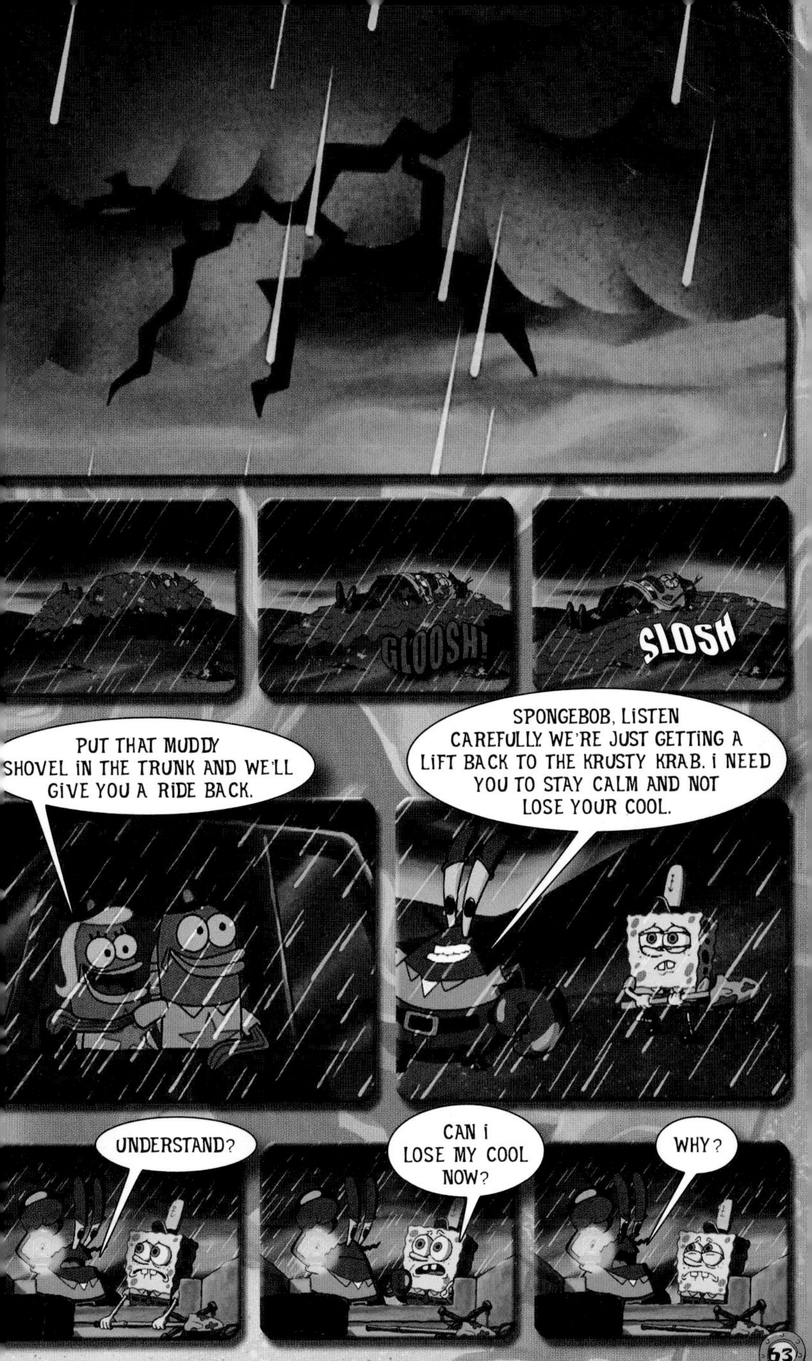
GLOOSH!
SLOSH
PUT THAT MUDDY SHOVEL IN THE TRUNK AND WE'LL GIVE YOU A RIDE BACK.
SPONGEBOB, LISTEN CAREFULLY. WE'RE JUST GETTING A LIFT BACK TO THE KRUSTY KRAB. I NEED YOU TO STAY CALM AND NOT LOSE YOUR COOL.
UNDERSTAND?
CAN I LOSE MY COOL NOW?
WHY?

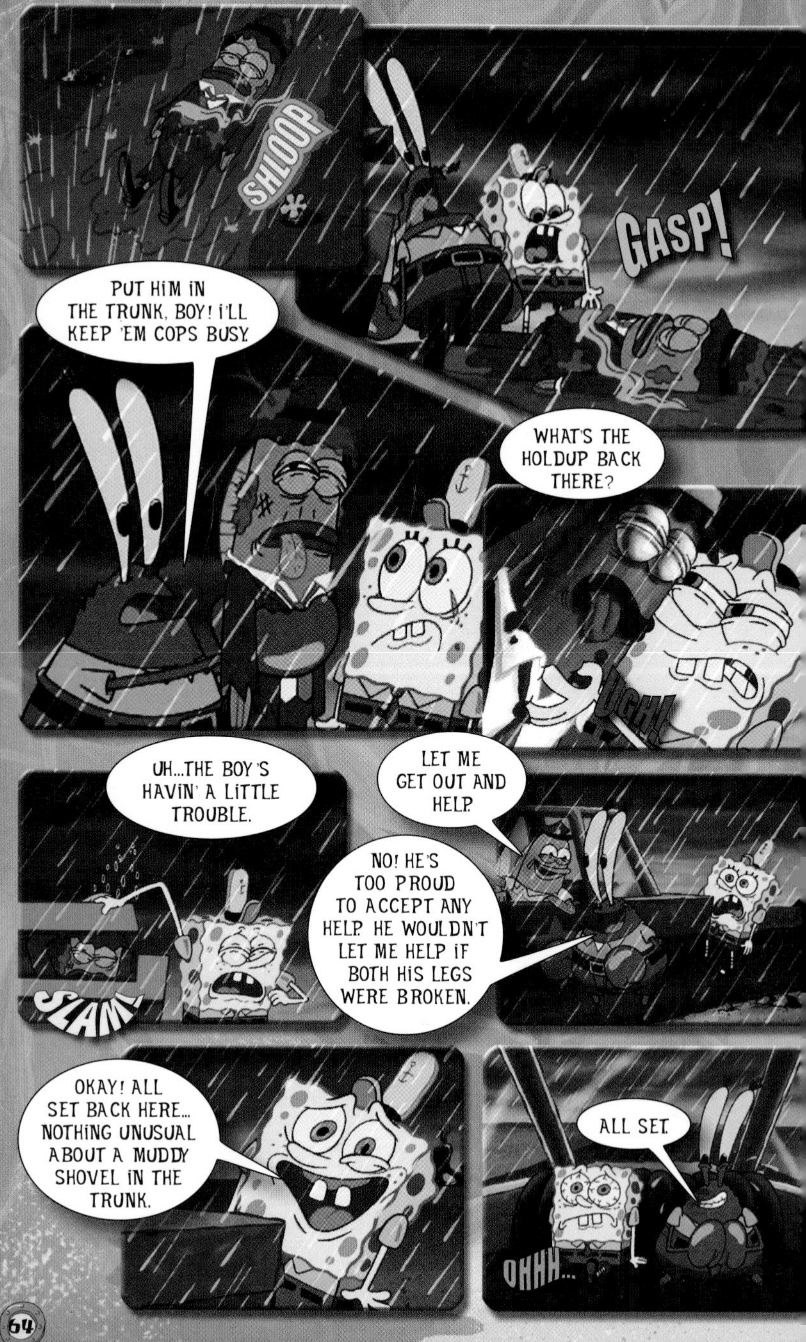
SHLOOP
GASP!
PUT HIM IN THE TRUNK, BOY! I'LL KEEP 'EM COPS BUSY.
WHAT'S THE HOLDUP BACK THERE?
UGH!
UH...THE BOY'S HAVIN' A LITTLE TROUBLE.
LET ME GET OUT AND HELP.
NO! HE'S TOO PROUD TO ACCEPT ANY HELP. HE WOULDN'T LET ME HELP IF BOTH HIS LEGS WERE BROKEN.
SLAM!
OKAY! ALL SET BACK HERE... NOTHING UNUSUAL ABOUT A MUDDY SHOVEL IN THE TRUNK.
ALL SET.
OHHH...

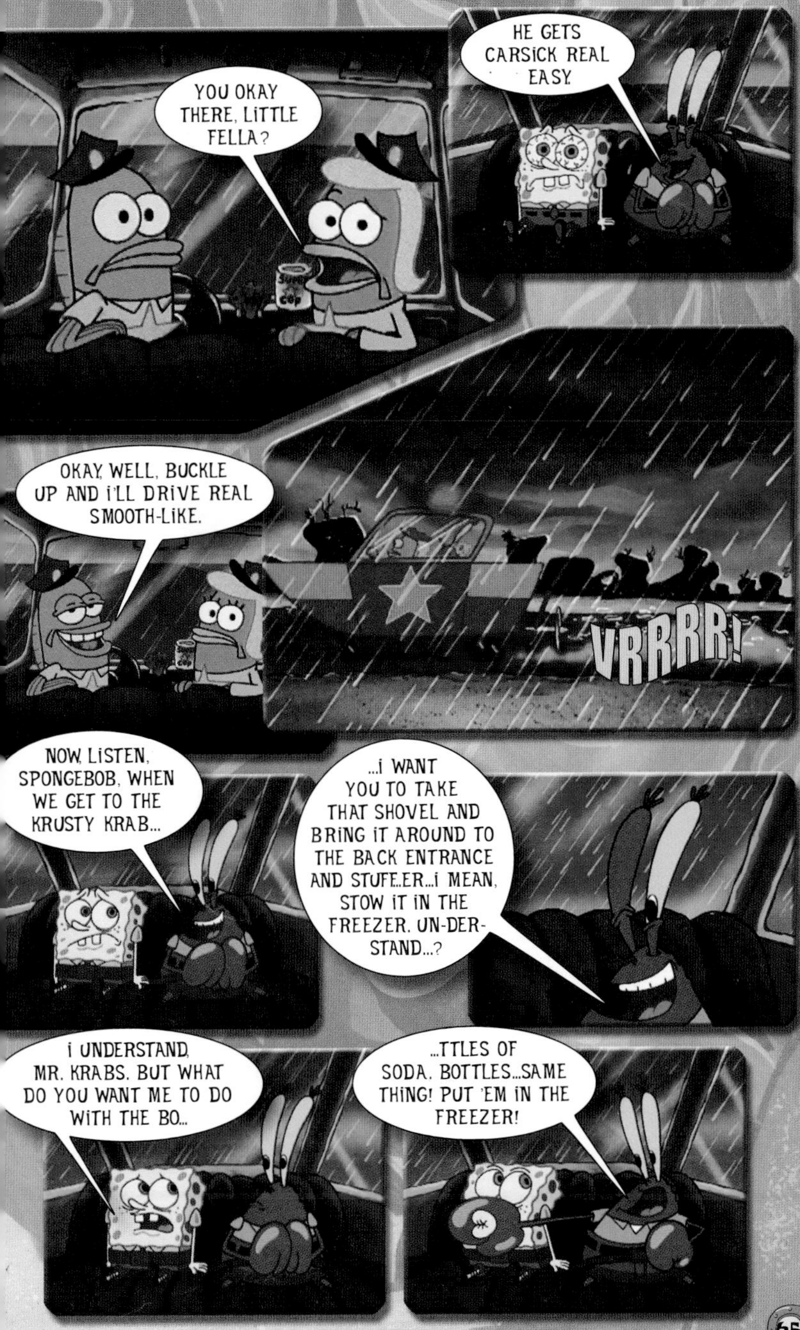
YOU OKAY THERE, LITTLE FELLA?
HE GETS CARSICK REAL EASY.
OKAY, WELL, BUCKLE UP AND I'LL DRIVE REAL SMOOTH-LIKE.
VRRRR!
NOW, LISTEN, SPONGEBOB, WHEN WE GET TO THE KRUSTY KRAB...
...I WANT YOU TO TAKE THAT SHOVEL AND BRING IT AROUND TO THE BACK ENTRANCE AND STUFF...ER...I MEAN, STOW IT IN THE FREEZER. UN-DER-STAND...?
I UNDERSTAND, MR. KRABS. BUT WHAT DO YOU WANT ME TO DO WITH THE BO...
...TTLES OF SODA. BOTTLES...SAME THING! PUT 'EM IN THE FREEZER!

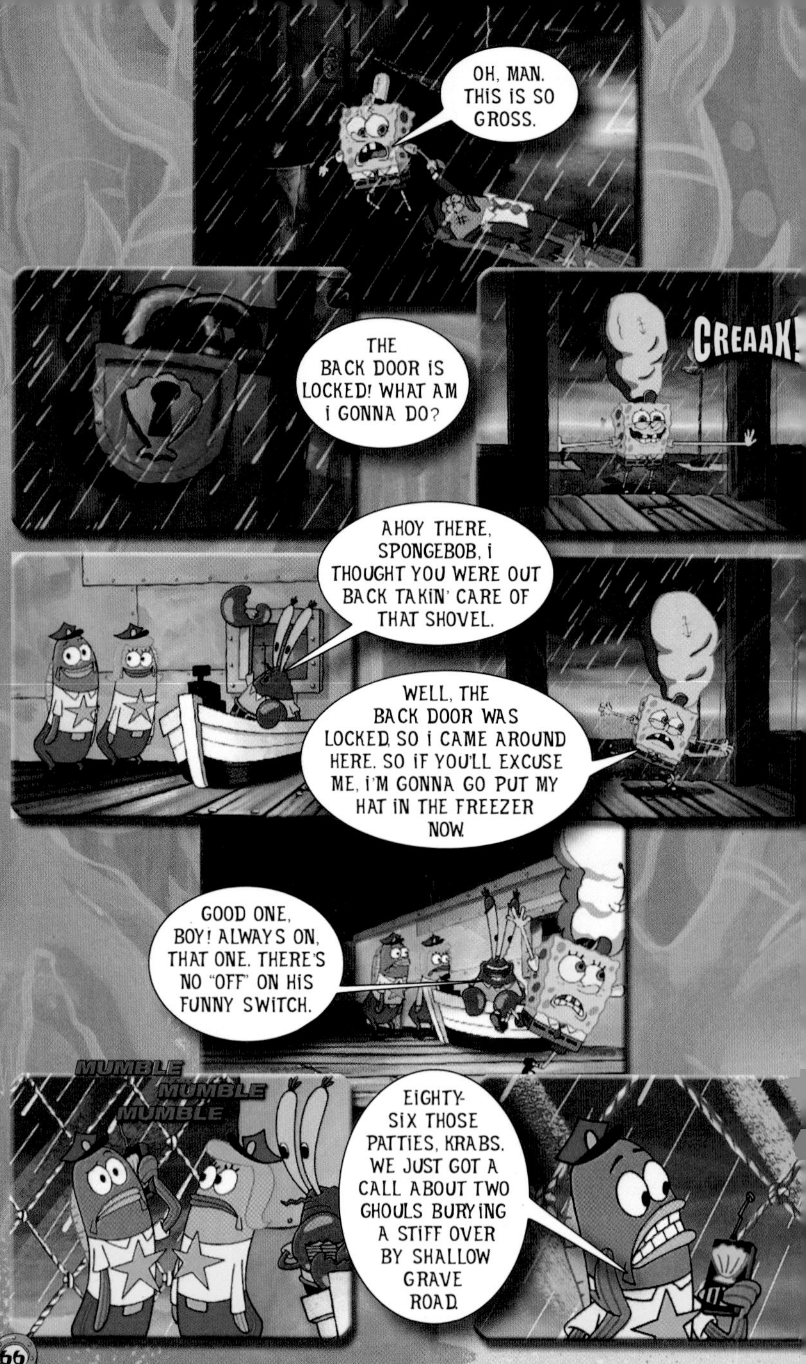
OH, MAN. THIS IS SO GROSS.
THE BACK DOOR IS LOCKED! WHAT AM I GONNA DO?
CREAAK!
AHOY THERE, SPONGEBOB, I THOUGHT YOU WERE OUT BACK TAKIN' CARE OF THAT SHOVEL.
WELL, THE BACK DOOR WAS LOCKED, SO I CAME AROUND HERE. SO IF YOU'LL EXCUSE ME, I'M GONNA GO PUT MY HAT IN THE FREEZER NOW.
GOOD ONE, BOY! ALWAYS ON, THAT ONE. THERE'S NO "OFF" ON HIS FUNNY SWITCH.
MUMBLE MUMBLE MUMBLE
EIGHTY-SIX THOSE PATTIES, KRABS. WE JUST GOT A CALL ABOUT TWO GHOULS BURYING A STIFF OVER BY SHALLOW GRAVE ROAD.

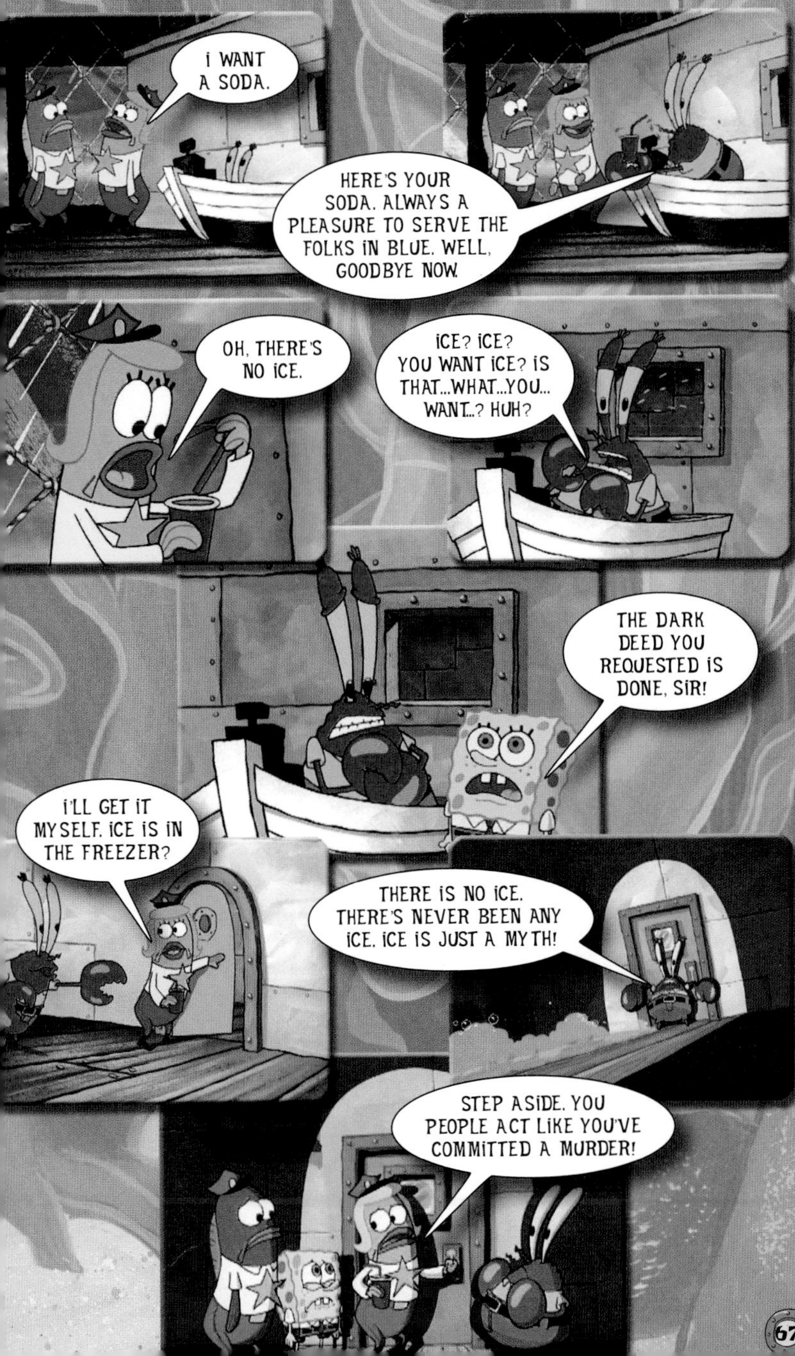
I WANT A SODA.
HERE'S YOUR SODA. ALWAYS A PLEASURE TO SERVE THE FOLKS IN BLUE. WELL, GOODBYE NOW.
OH, THERE'S NO ICE.
ICE? ICE? YOU WANT ICE? IS THAT...WHAT...YOU... WANT...? HUH?
THE DARK DEED YOU REQUESTED IS DONE, SIR!
I'LL GET IT MYSELF. ICE IS IN THE FREEZER?
THERE IS NO ICE. THERE'S NEVER BEEN ANY ICE. ICE IS JUST A MYTH!
STEP ASIDE. YOU PEOPLE ACT LIKE YOU'VE COMMITTED A MURDER!

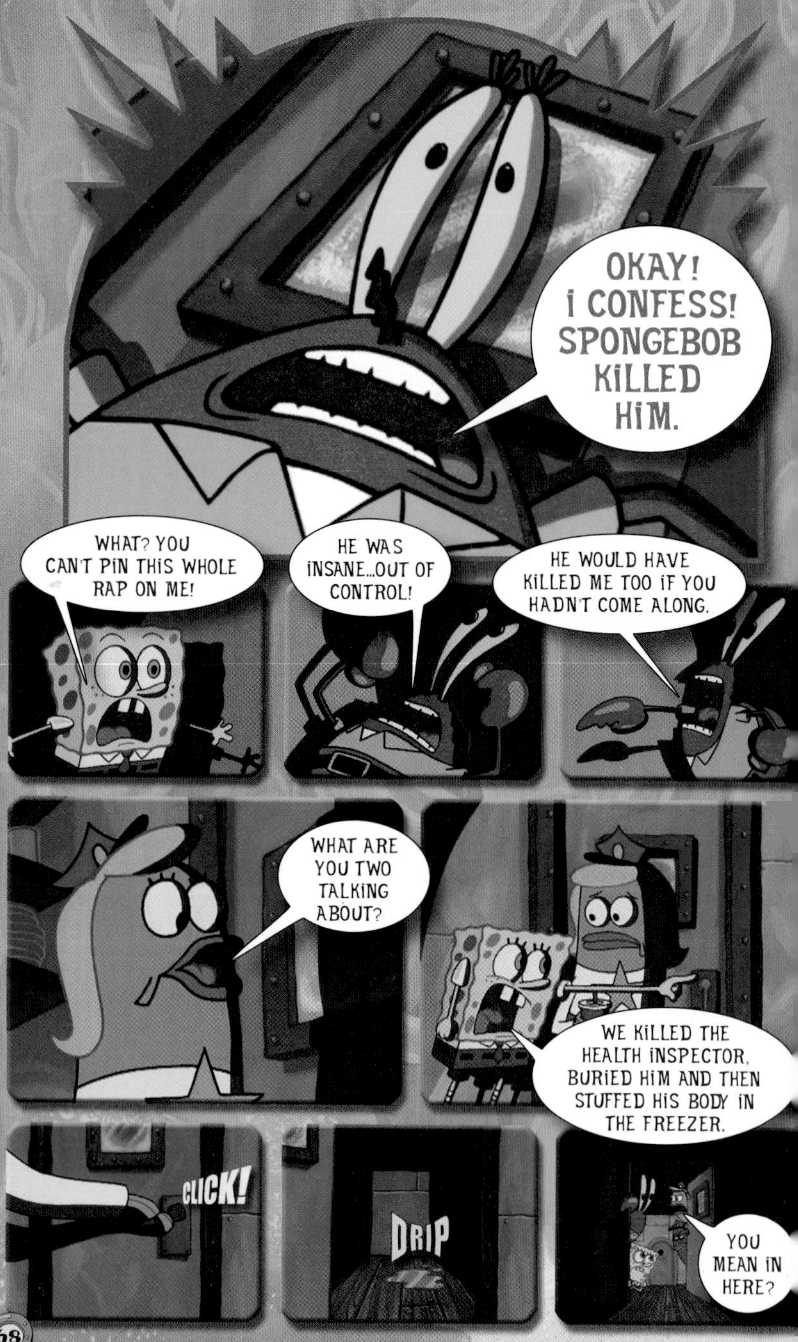

OKAY! I CONFESS! SPONGEBOB KILLED HIM.
WHAT? YOU CAN'T PIN THIS WHOLE RAP ON ME!
HE WAS INSANE...OUT OF CONTROL!
HE WOULD HAVE KILLED ME TOO IF YOU HADN'T COME ALONG.
WHAT ARE YOU TWO TALKING ABOUT?
WE KILLED THE HEALTH INSPECTOR, BURIED HIM AND THEN STUFFED HIS BODY IN THE FREEZER.
CLICK!
DRIP
YOU MEAN IN HERE?

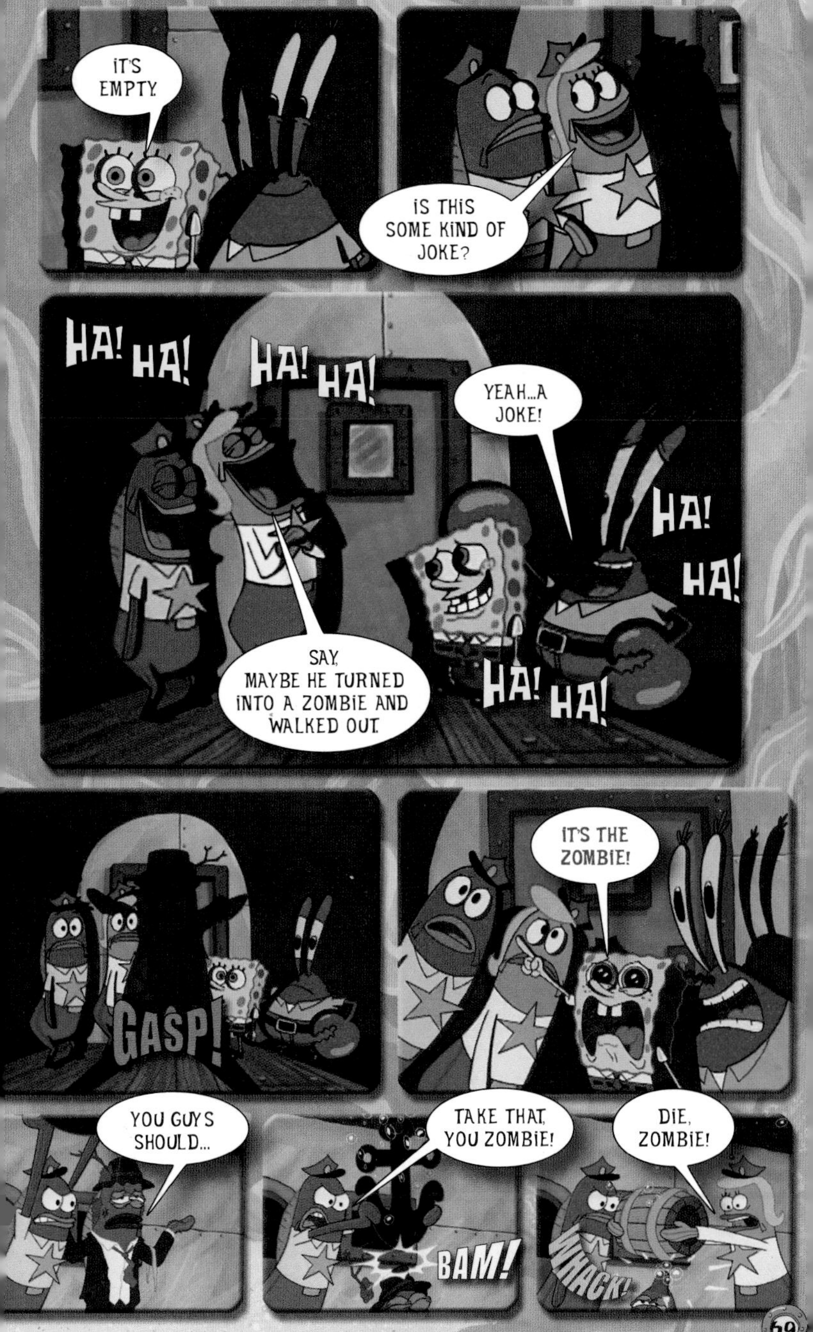

IT'S EMPTY.
IS THIS SOME KIND OF JOKE?
HA! HA!
HA! HA!
YEAH...A JOKE!
HA! HA!
SAY, MAYBE HE TURNED INTO A ZOMBIE AND WALKED OUT.
HA! HA!
GASP!
IT'S THE ZOMBIE!
YOU GUYS SHOULD...
TAKE THAT, YOU ZOMBIE!
BAM!
DIE, ZOMBIE!
WHACK!

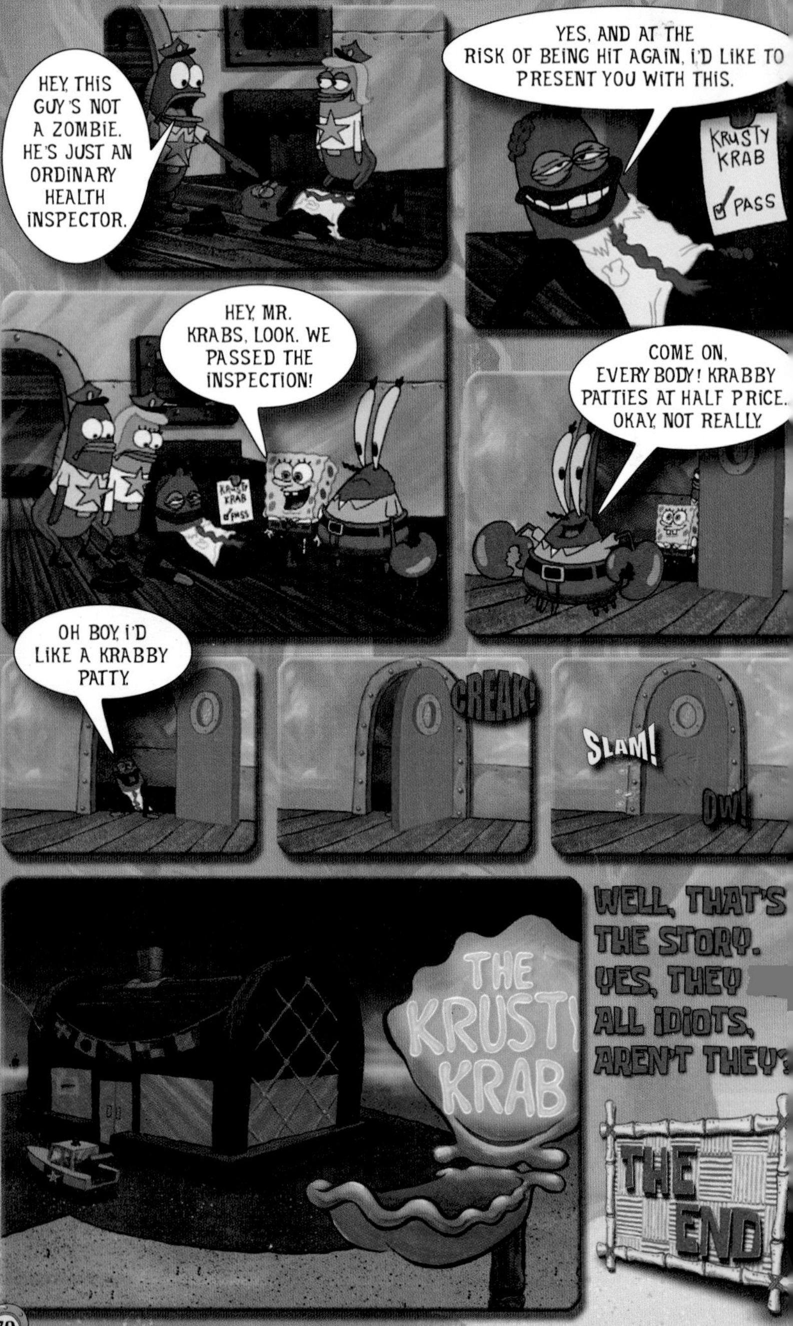
HEY, THIS GUY'S NOT A ZOMBIE. HE'S JUST AN ORDINARY HEALTH INSPECTOR.
YES, AND AT THE RISK OF BEING HIT AGAIN, I'D LIKE TO PRESENT YOU WITH THIS.
KRUSTY KRAB
PASS
HEY, MR. KRABS, LOOK. WE PASSED THE INSPECTION!
COME ON, EVERY BODY! KRABBY PATTIES AT HALF PRICE. OKAY, NOT REALLY.
OH BOY, I'D LIKE A KRABBY PATTY.
CREAK!
SLAM!
OW!
THE KRUSTY KRAB
WELL, THAT'S THE STORY. YES, THEY
ALL IDIOTS, AREN'T THEY?
THE END

SPONGEBOB SQUAREPANTS

SUPERFRIENDS

by C.H. Greenblatt, Kaz
and Merriwether Williams

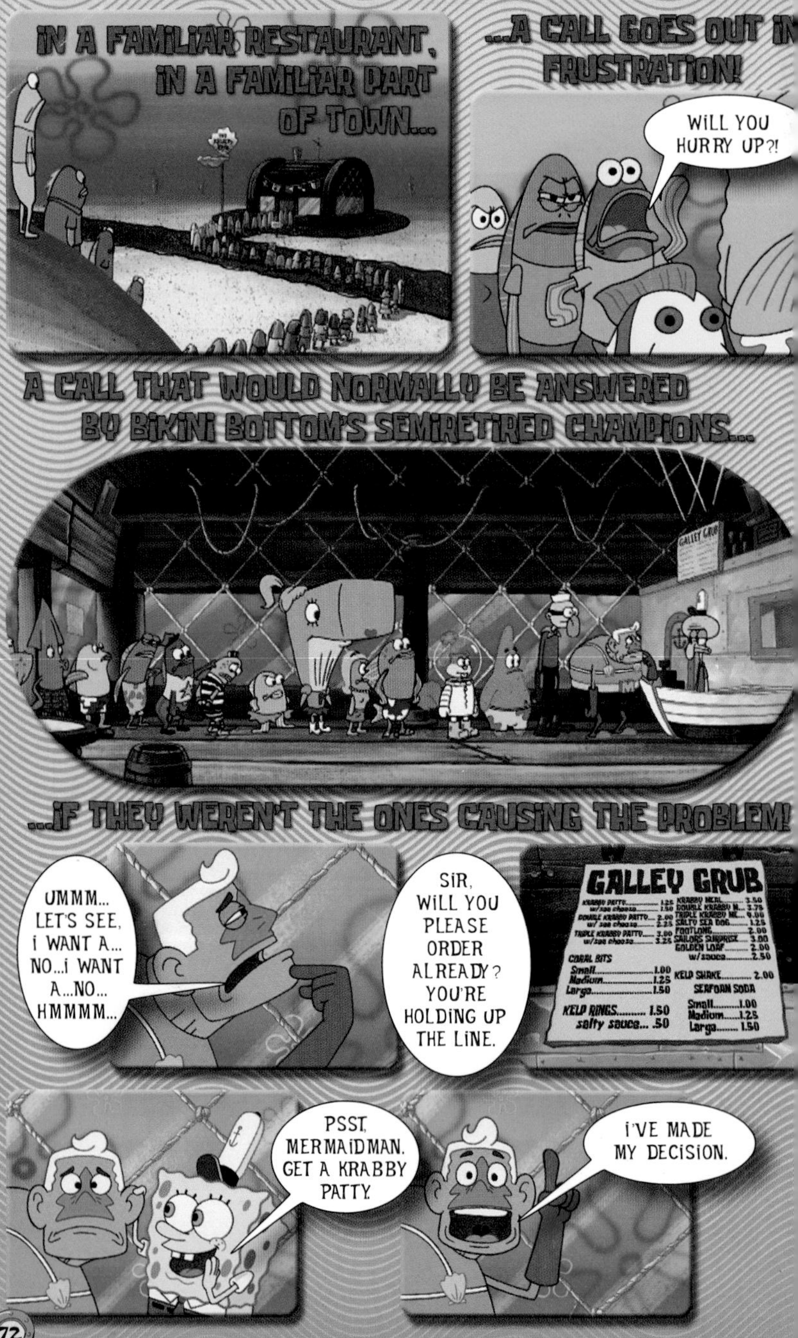
IN A FAMILIAR RESTAURANT, IN A FAMILIAR PART OF TOWN...
...A CALL GOES OUT IN FRUSTRATION!
WILL YOU HURRY UP?!
A CALL THAT WOULD NORMALLY BE ANSWERED BY BIKINI BOTTOM'S SEMIRETIRED CHAMPIONS...
...IF THEY WEREN'T THE ONES CAUSING THE PROBLEM!
UMMM... LET'S SEE, I WANT A... NO...I WANT A...NO... HMMMM...
SIR, WILL YOU PLEASE ORDER ALREADY? YOU'RE HOLDING UP THE LINE.
GALLEY GRUB
CORAL BITS
Small.......1.00
Medium.......1.25
Large.......1.50
KELP RINGS......... 1.50
salty sauce... .50
KELP SHAKE.......... 2.00
SEAFOAM SODA
Small.........1.00
Medium.....1.25
Large...... 1.50
PSST, MERMAIDMAN. GET A KRABBY PATTY.
I'VE MADE MY DECISION.

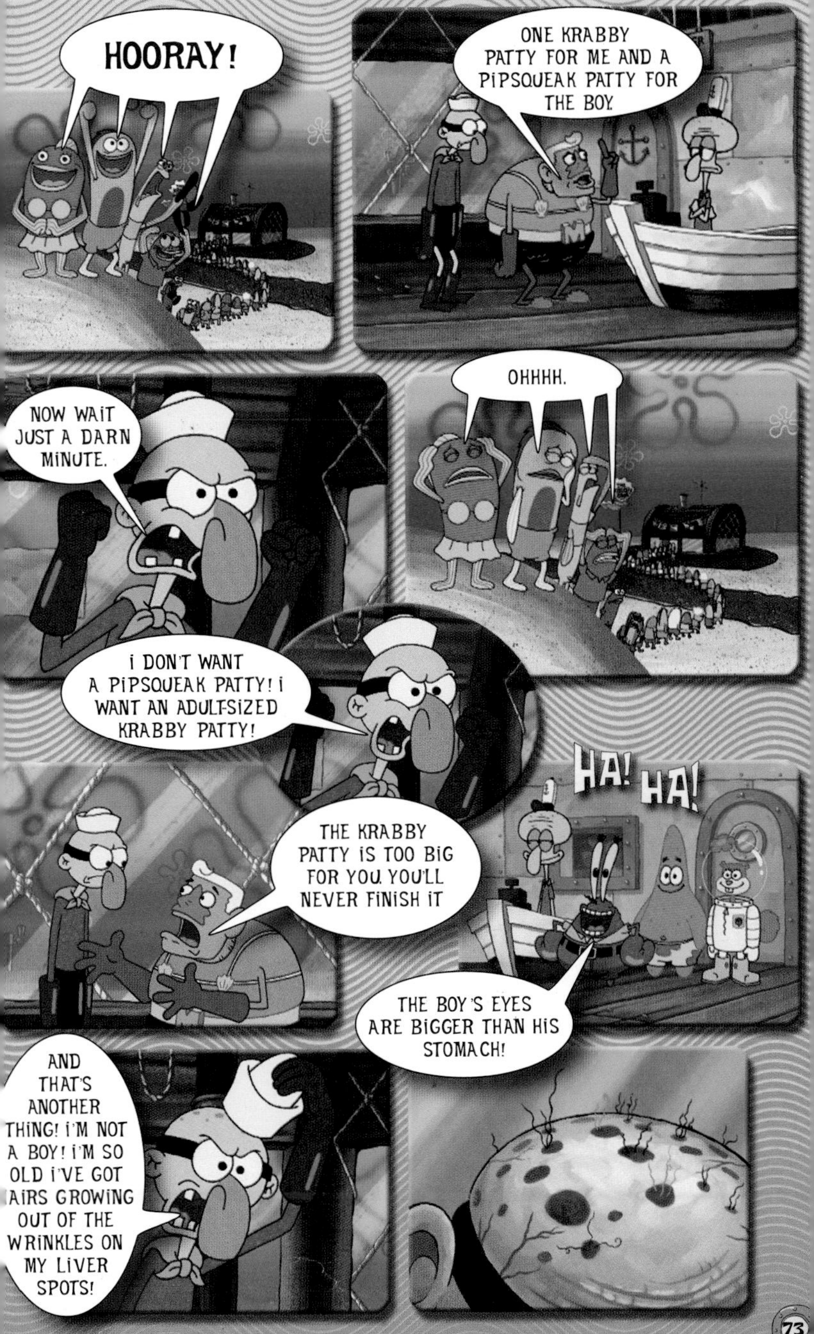
HOORAY!
ONE KRABBY PATTY FOR ME AND A PIPSQUEAK PATTY FOR THE BOY.
NOW WAIT JUST A DARN MINUTE.
OHHHH.
I DON'T WANT A PIPSQUEAK PATTY! I WANT AN ADULT-SIZED KRABBY PATTY!
THE KRABBY PATTY IS TOO BIG FOR YOU. YOU'LL NEVER FINISH IT
HA! HA!
THE BOY'S EYES ARE BIGGER THAN HIS STOMACH!
AND THAT'S ANOTHER THING! I'M NOT A BOY! I'M SO OLD I'VE GOT AIRS GROWING OUT OF THE WRINKLES ON MY LIVER SPOTS!

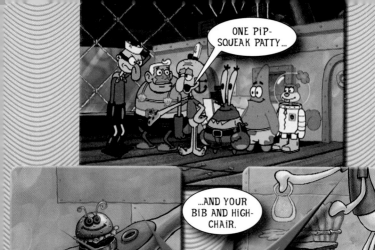

ONE PIP-SQUEAK PATTY...

...AND YOUR BIB AND HIGH-CHAIR.

I'M SIXTY-EIGHT YEARS OLD AND I WANT A KRABBY PATTY!

YOUR PIP-SQUEAK IS GETTING COLD. SHALL I FEED YOU?

FEED THIS, OLD MAN!

SMACK!

OOOOHH...

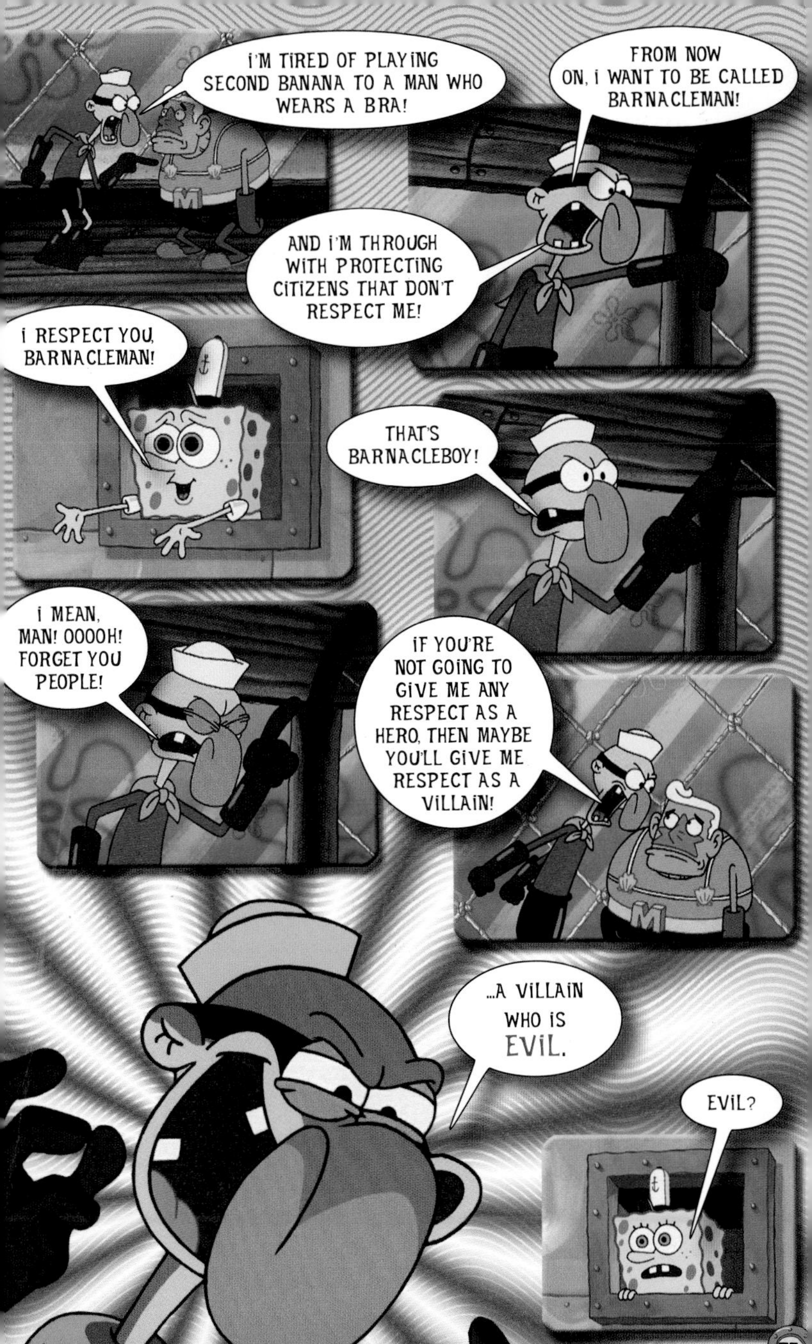
I'M TIRED OF PLAYING SECOND BANANA TO A MAN WHO WEARS A BRA!
FROM NOW ON, I WANT TO BE CALLED BARNACLEMAN!
AND I'M THROUGH WITH PROTECTING CITIZENS THAT DON'T RESPECT ME!
I RESPECT YOU, BARNACLEMAN!
THAT'S BARNACLEBOY!
I MEAN, MAN! OOOOH! FORGET YOU PEOPLE!
IF YOU'RE NOT GOING TO GIVE ME ANY RESPECT AS A HERO, THEN MAYBE YOU'LL GIVE ME RESPECT AS A VILLAIN!
...A VILLAIN WHO IS EVIL.
EVIL?

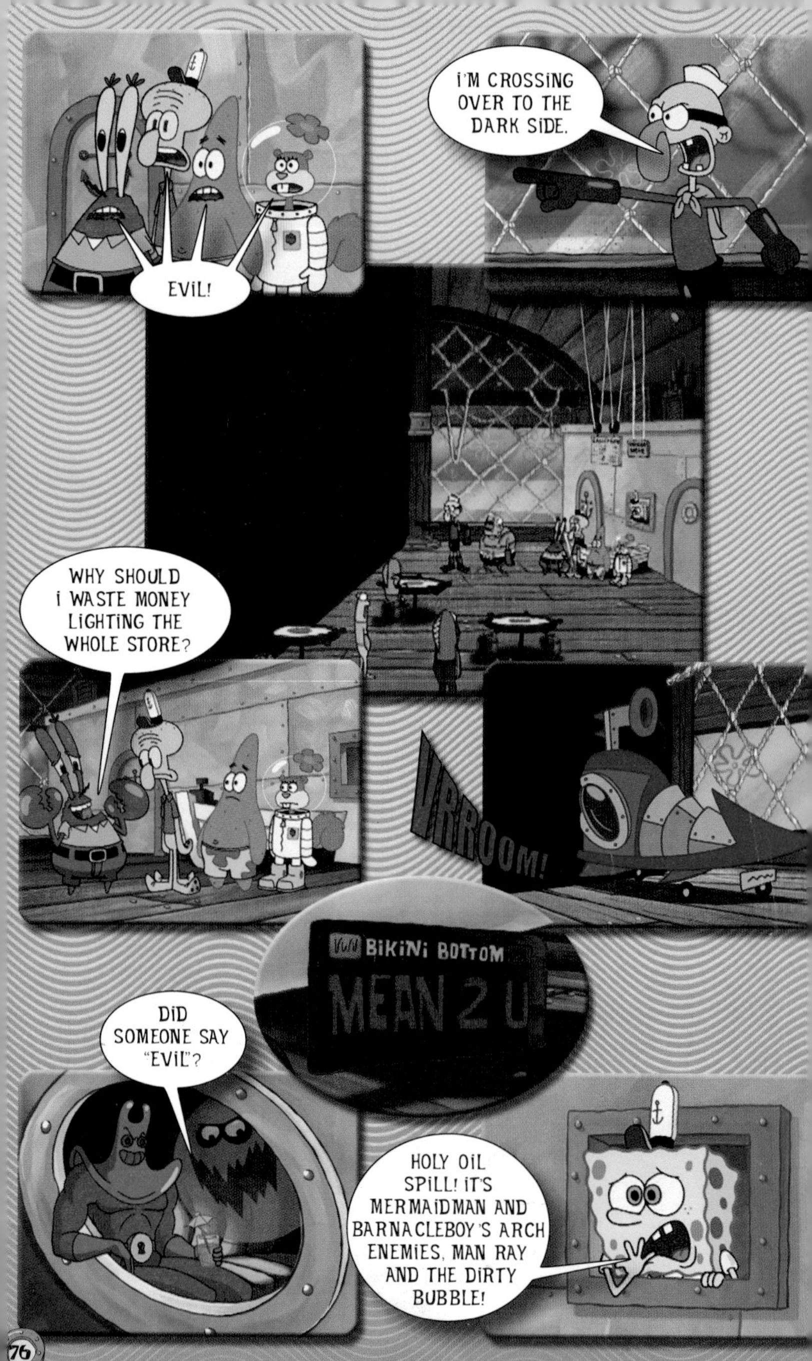
EVIL!
I'M CROSSING OVER TO THE DARK SIDE.
WHY SHOULD I WASTE MONEY LIGHTING THE WHOLE STORE?
VRROOM!
BIKINI BOTTOM
MEAN 2 U
DID SOMEONE SAY "EVIL"?
HOLY OIL SPILL! IT'S MERMAIDMAN AND BARNACLEBOY'S ARCH ENEMIES, MAN RAY AND THE DIRTY BUBBLE!

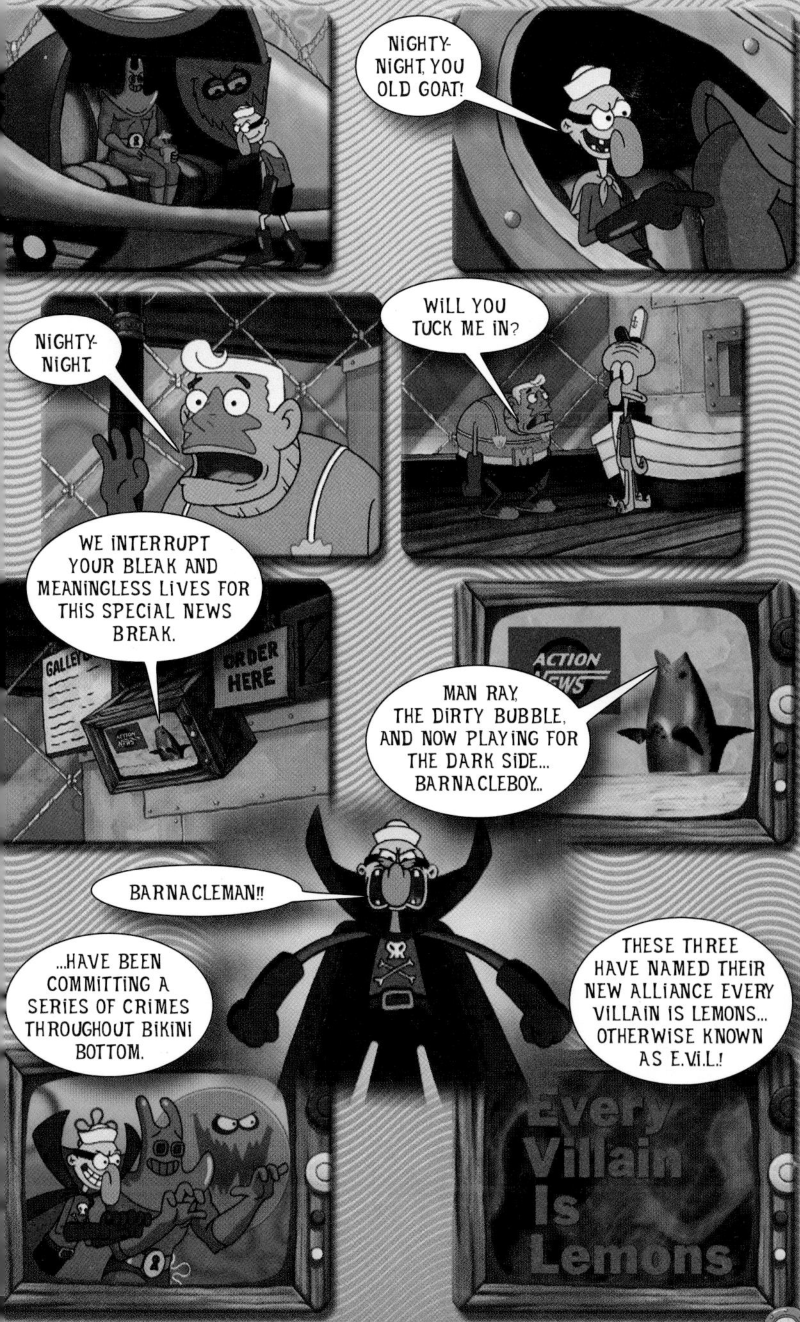
NIGHTY-NIGHT, YOU OLD GOAT!
NIGHTY-NIGHT.
WILL YOU TUCK ME IN?
WE INTERRUPT YOUR BLEAK AND MEANINGLESS LIVES FOR THIS SPECIAL NEWS BREAK.
GALLEY
ORDER HERE
ACTION NEWS
MAN RAY, THE DIRTY BUBBLE, AND NOW PLAYING FOR THE DARK SIDE... BARNACLEBOY...
BARNACLEMAN!!
...HAVE BEEN COMMITTING A SERIES OF CRIMES THROUGHOUT BIKINI BOTTOM.
THESE THREE HAVE NAMED THEIR NEW ALLIANCE EVERY VILLAIN IS LEMONS... OTHERWISE KNOWN AS E.V.I.L.!
Every Villain Is Lemons

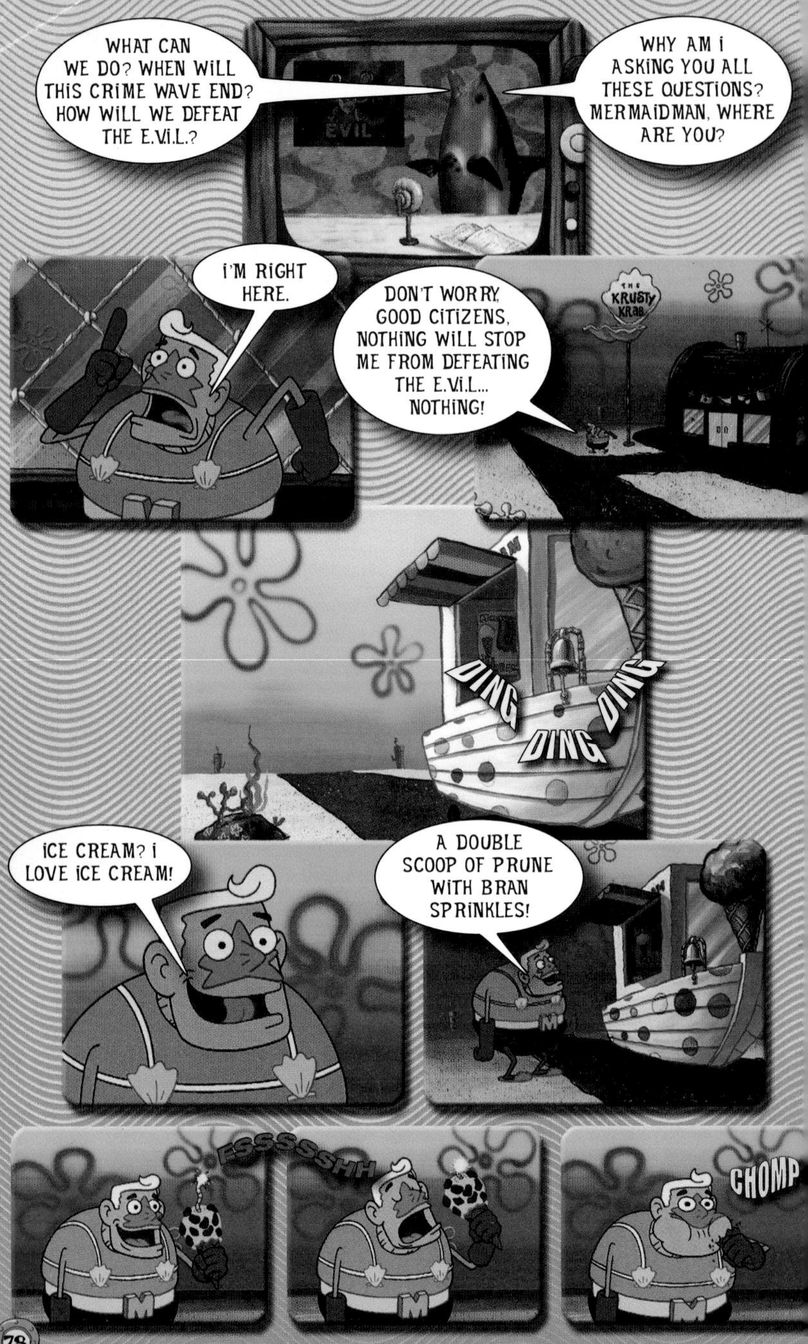
WHAT CAN WE DO? WHEN WILL THIS CRIME WAVE END? HOW WILL WE DEFEAT THE E.V.I.L.?
EVIL
WHY AM I ASKING YOU ALL THESE QUESTIONS? MERMAIDMAN, WHERE ARE YOU?
I'M RIGHT HERE.
DON'T WORRY, GOOD CITIZENS, NOTHING WILL STOP ME FROM DEFEATING THE E.V.I.L... NOTHING!
THE KRUSTY KRAB
DING
DING
DING
ICE CREAM? I LOVE ICE CREAM!
A DOUBLE SCOOP OF PRUNE WITH BRAN SPRINKLES!
FSSSSSSHH
CHOMP

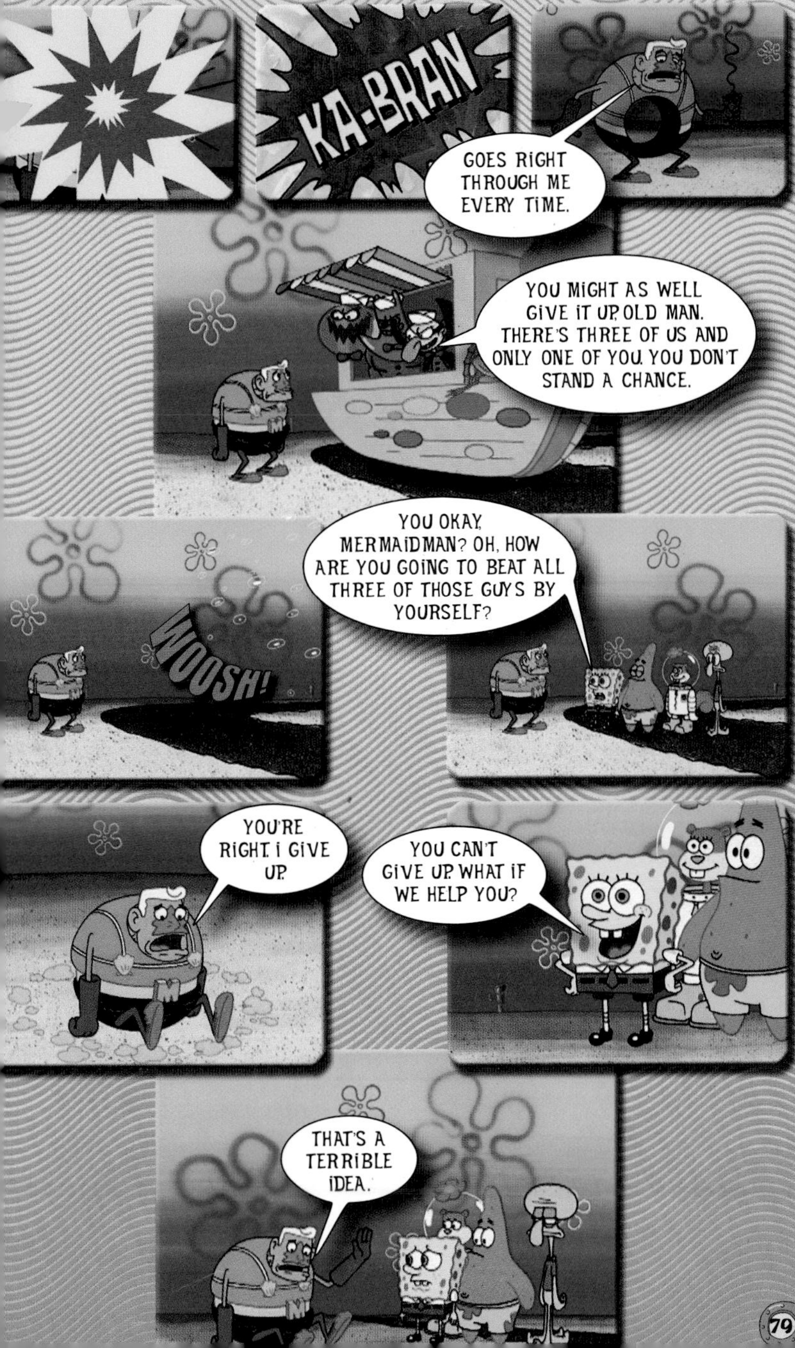
KA-BRAN
GOES RIGHT THROUGH ME EVERY TIME.
YOU MIGHT AS WELL GIVE IT UP, OLD MAN. THERE'S THREE OF US AND ONLY ONE OF YOU. YOU DON'T STAND A CHANCE.
WOOSH!
YOU OKAY, MERMAIDMAN? OH, HOW ARE YOU GOING TO BEAT ALL THREE OF THOSE GUYS BY YOURSELF?
YOU'RE RIGHT. I GIVE UP.
YOU CAN'T GIVE UP. WHAT IF WE HELP YOU?
THAT'S A TERRIBLE IDEA.

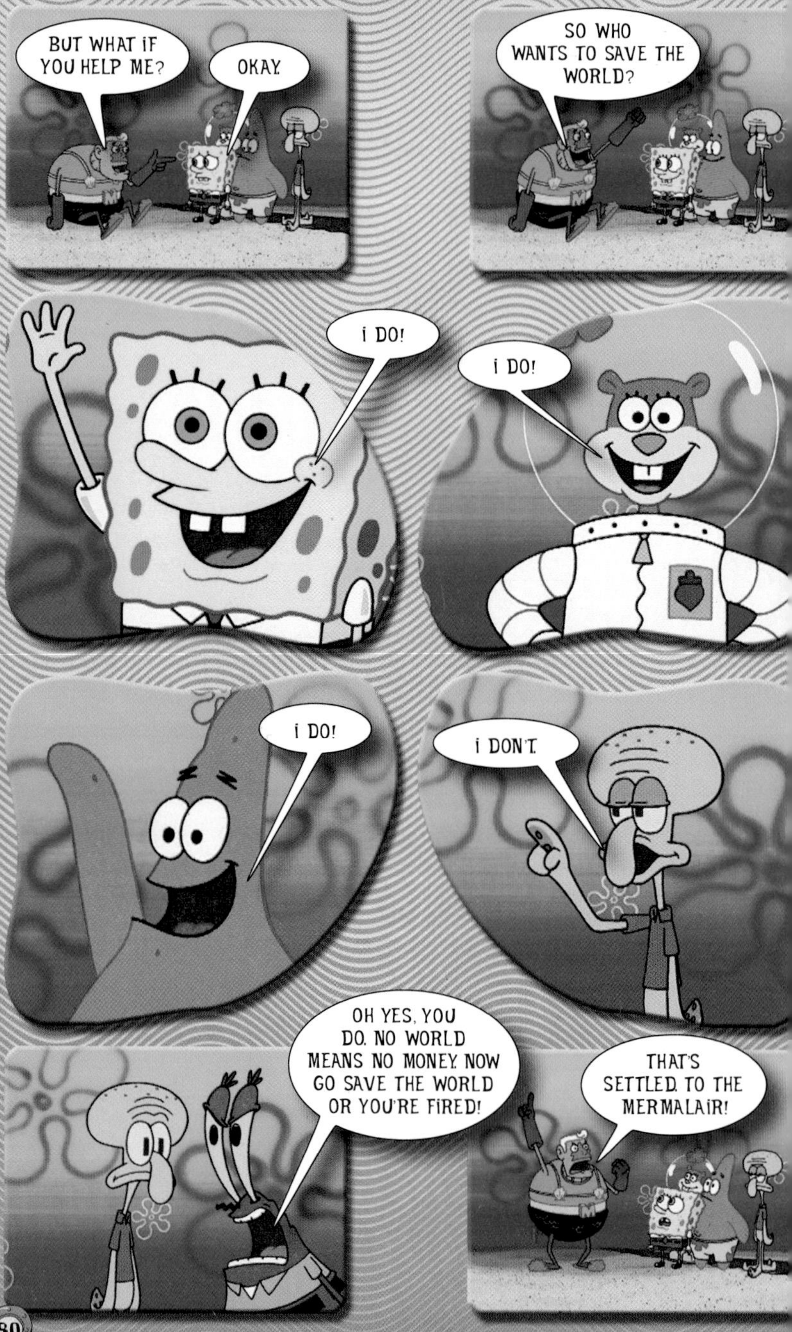
BUT WHAT IF YOU HELP ME?
OKAY.
SO WHO WANTS TO SAVE THE WORLD?
I DO!
I DO!
I DO!
I DON'T.
OH YES, YOU DO. NO WORLD MEANS NO MONEY. NOW GO SAVE THE WORLD OR YOU'RE FIRED!
THAT'S SETTLED. TO THE MERMALAIR!

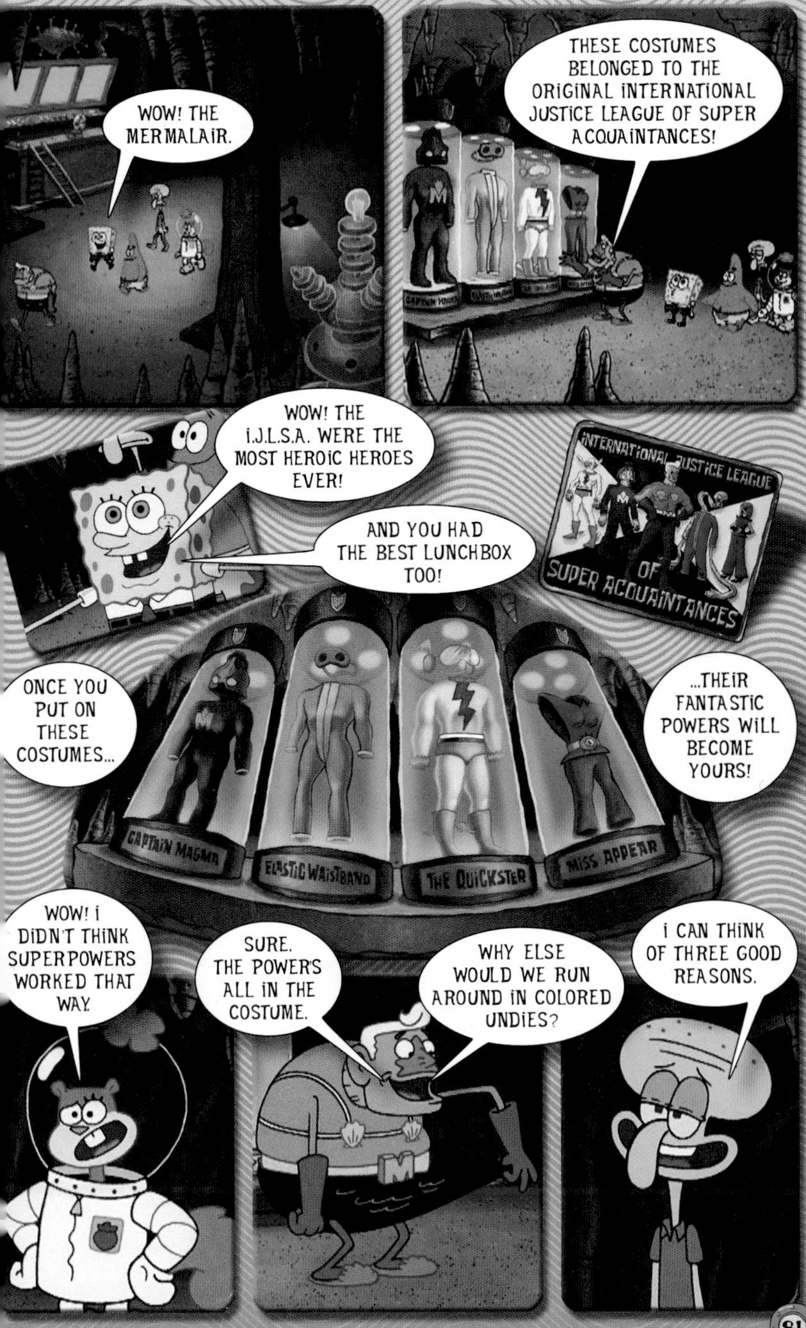
WOW! THE MERMALAIR.
THESE COSTUMES BELONGED TO THE ORIGINAL INTERNATIONAL JUSTICE LEAGUE OF SUPER ACQUAINTANCES!
WOW! THE I.J.L.S.A. WERE THE MOST HEROIC HEROES EVER!
AND YOU HAD THE BEST LUNCHBOX TOO!
INTERNATIONAL JUSTICE LEAGUE OF SUPER ACQUAINTANCES
ONCE YOU PUT ON THESE COSTUMES...
...THEIR FANTASTIC POWERS WILL BECOME YOURS!
CAPTAIN MAGMA
ELASTIC WAISTBAND
THE QUICKSTER
MISS APPEAR
WOW! I DIDN'T THINK SUPERPOWERS WORKED THAT WAY.
SURE. THE POWER'S ALL IN THE COSTUME.
WHY ELSE WOULD WE RUN AROUND IN COLORED UNDIES?
I CAN THINK OF THREE GOOD REASONS.

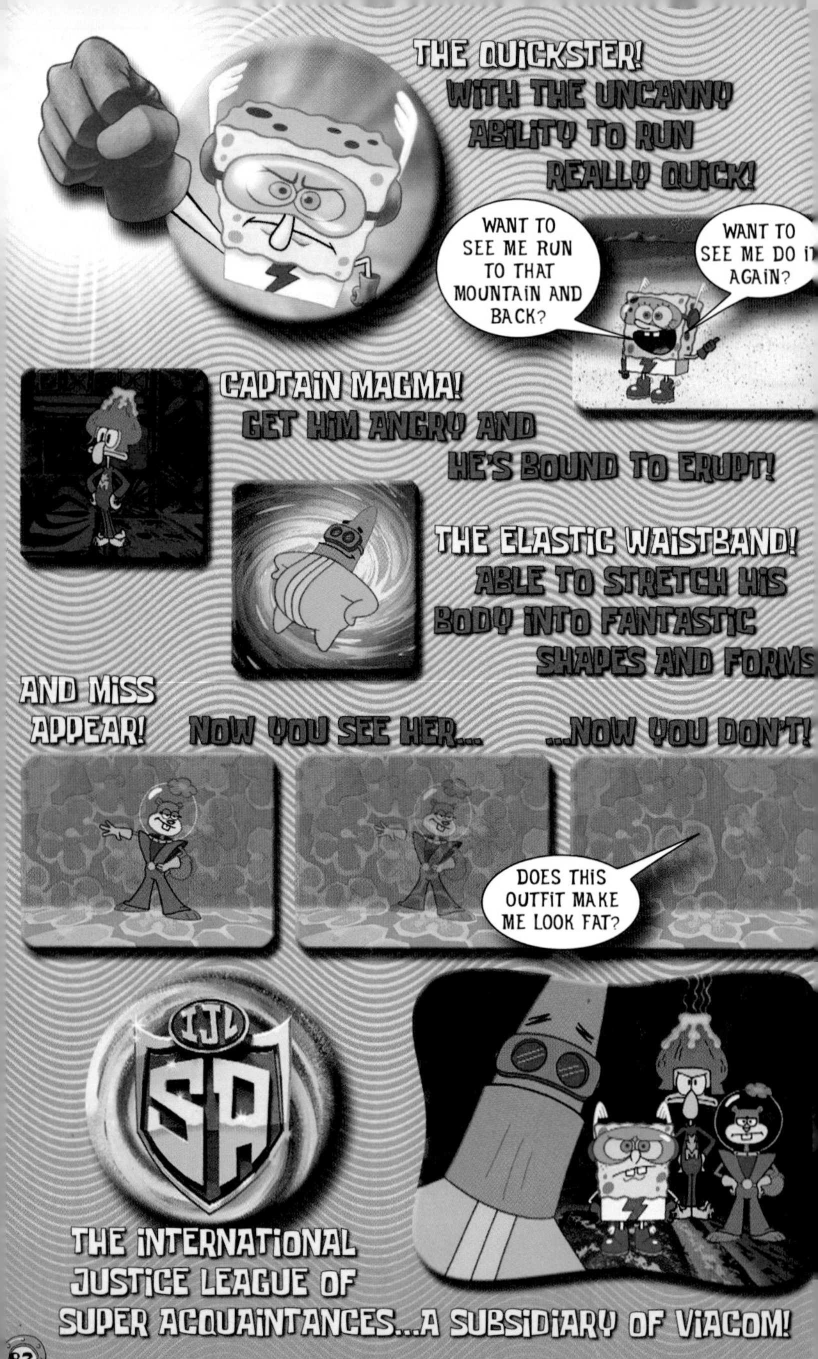
THE QUICKSTER! WITH THE UNCANNY ABILITY TO RUN REALLY QUICK!
WANT TO SEE ME RUN TO THAT MOUNTAIN AND BACK?
WANT TO SEE ME DO IT AGAIN?
CAPTAIN MAGMA! GET HIM ANGRY AND HE'S BOUND TO ERUPT!
THE ELASTIC WAISTBAND! ABLE TO STRETCH HIS BODY INTO FANTASTIC SHAPES AND FORMS
AND MISS APPEAR!
NOW YOU SEE HER...
...NOW YOU DON'T!
DOES THIS OUTFIT MAKE ME LOOK FAT?
IJL
SA
THE INTERNATIONAL JUSTICE LEAGUE OF SUPER ACQUAINTANCES...A SUBSIDIARY OF VIACOM!

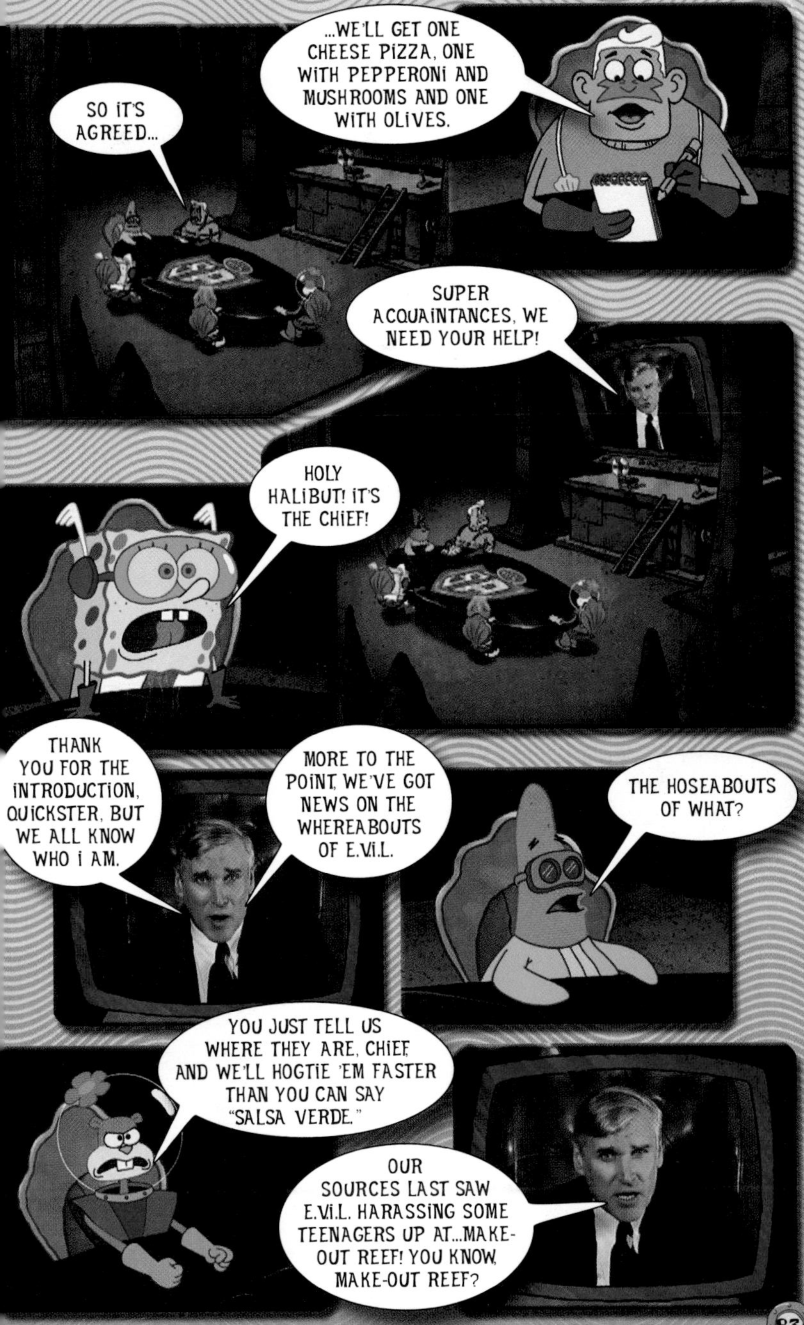

SO IT'S AGREED...
...WE'LL GET ONE CHEESE PIZZA, ONE WITH PEPPERONI AND MUSHROOMS AND ONE WITH OLIVES.
SUPER ACQUAINTANCES, WE NEED YOUR HELP!
HOLY HALIBUT! IT'S THE CHIEF!
THANK YOU FOR THE INTRODUCTION, QUICKSTER, BUT WE ALL KNOW WHO I AM.
MORE TO THE POINT, WE'VE GOT NEWS ON THE WHEREABOUTS OF E.V.I.L.
THE HOSEABOUTS OF WHAT?
YOU JUST TELL US WHERE THEY ARE, CHIEF, AND WE'LL HOGTIE 'EM FASTER THAN YOU CAN SAY "SALSA VERDE."
OUR SOURCES LAST SAW E.V.I.L. HARASSING SOME TEENAGERS UP AT...MAKE-OUT REEF! YOU KNOW, MAKE-OUT REEF?

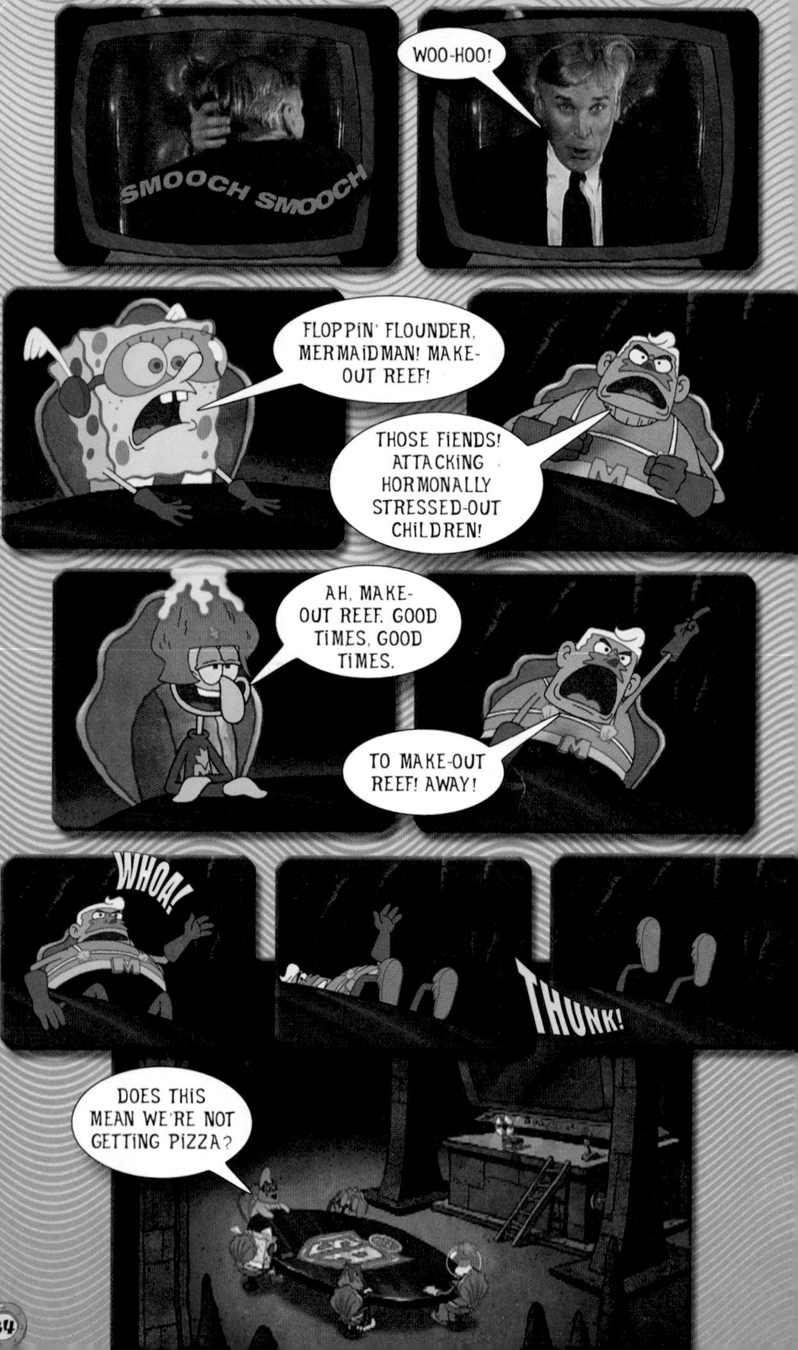
SMOOCH SMOOCH
WOO-HOO!
FLOPPIN' FLOUNDER, MERMAIDMAN! MAKE-OUT REEF!
THOSE FIENDS! ATTACKING HORMONALLY STRESSED-OUT CHILDREN!
AH, MAKE-OUT REEF. GOOD TIMES, GOOD TIMES.
TO MAKE-OUT REEF! AWAY!
WHOA!
THUNK!
DOES THIS MEAN WE'RE NOT GETTING PIZZA?

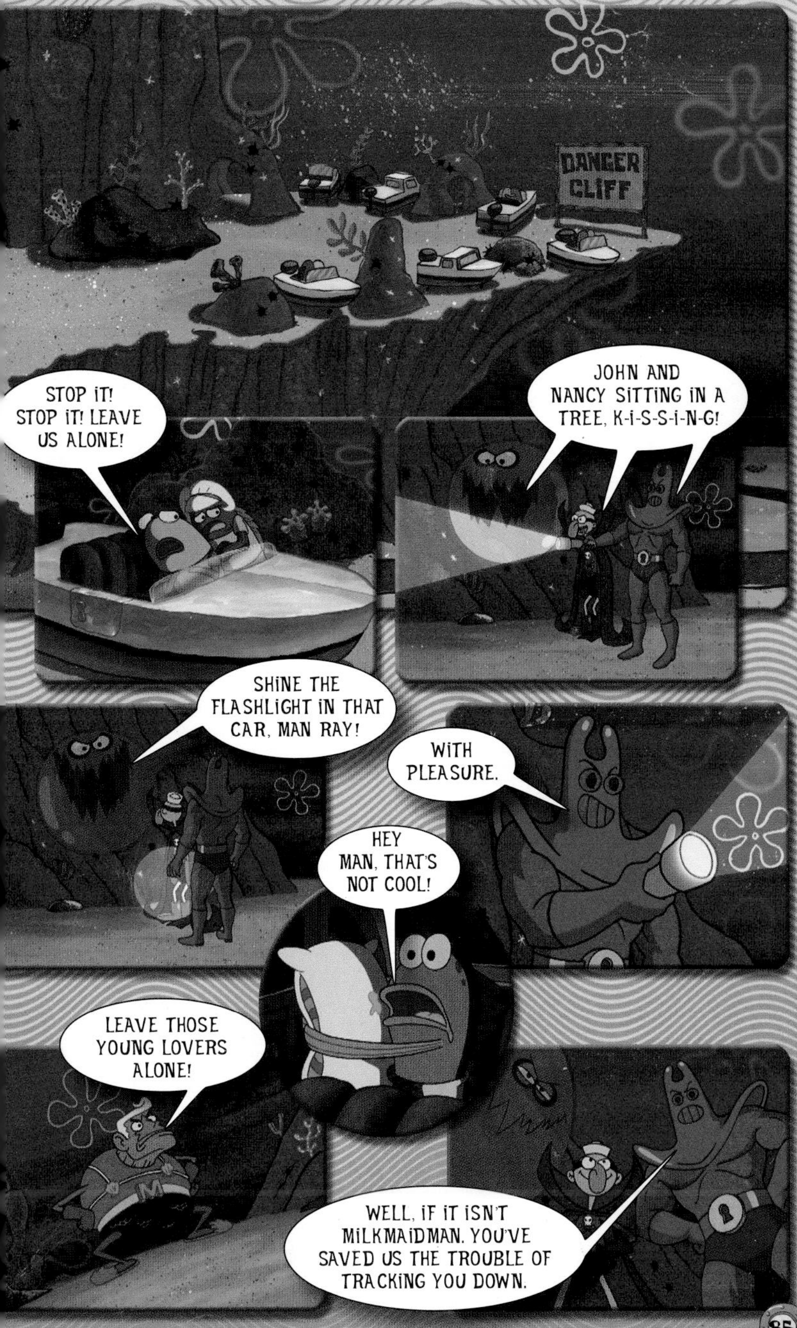
DANGER CLIFF
STOP IT! STOP IT! LEAVE US ALONE!
JOHN AND NANCY SITTING IN A TREE, K-I-S-S-I-N-G!
SHINE THE FLASHLIGHT IN THAT CAR, MAN RAY!
WITH PLEASURE.
HEY MAN, THAT'S NOT COOL!
LEAVE THOSE YOUNG LOVERS ALONE!
WELL, IF IT ISN'T MILKMAIDMAN. YOU'VE SAVED US THE TROUBLE OF TRACKING YOU DOWN.

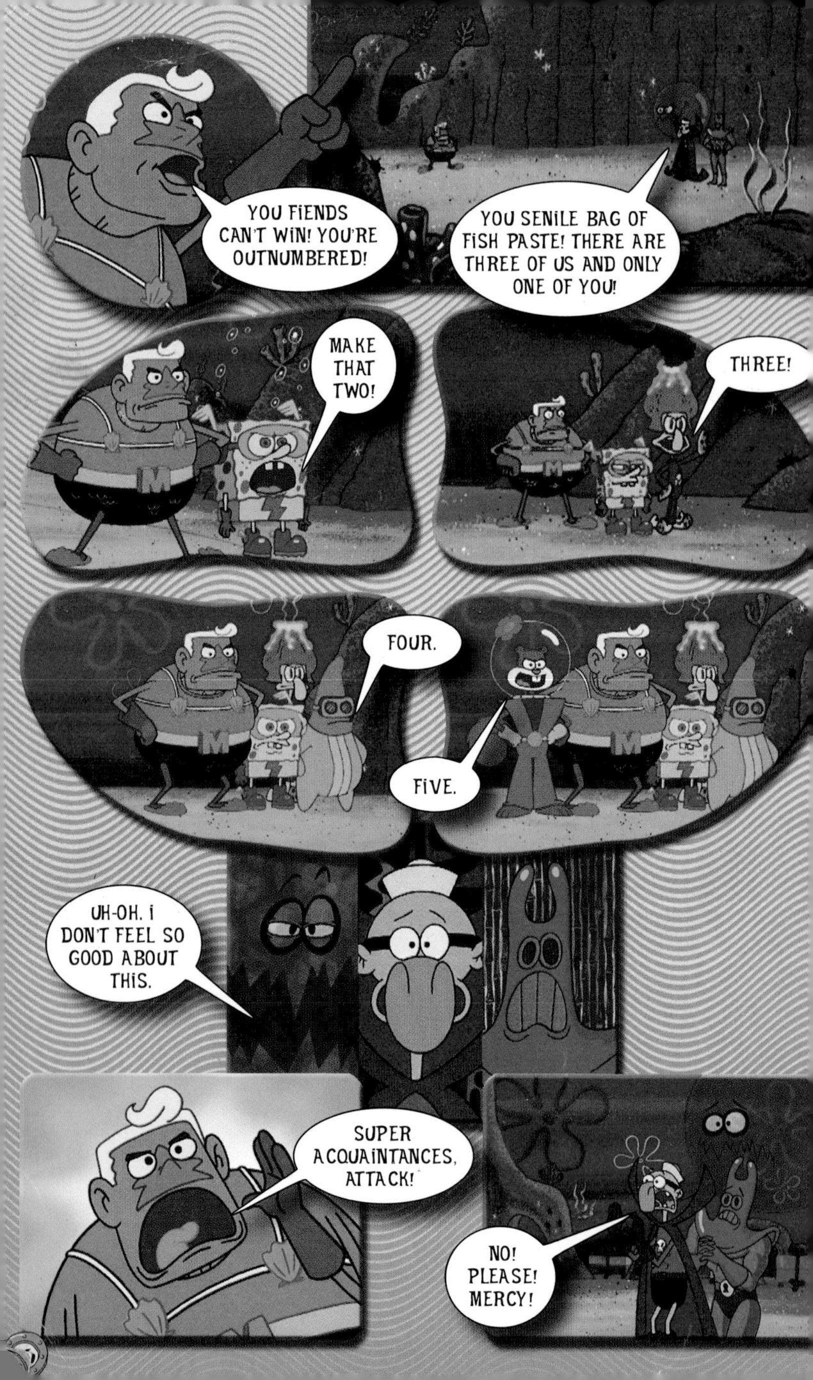
YOU FIENDS CAN'T WIN! YOU'RE OUTNUMBERED!
YOU SENILE BAG OF FISH PASTE! THERE ARE THREE OF US AND ONLY ONE OF YOU!
MAKE THAT TWO!
THREE!
FOUR.
FIVE.
UH-OH. I DON'T FEEL SO GOOD ABOUT THIS.
SUPER ACQUAINTANCES, ATTACK!
NO! PLEASE! MERCY!

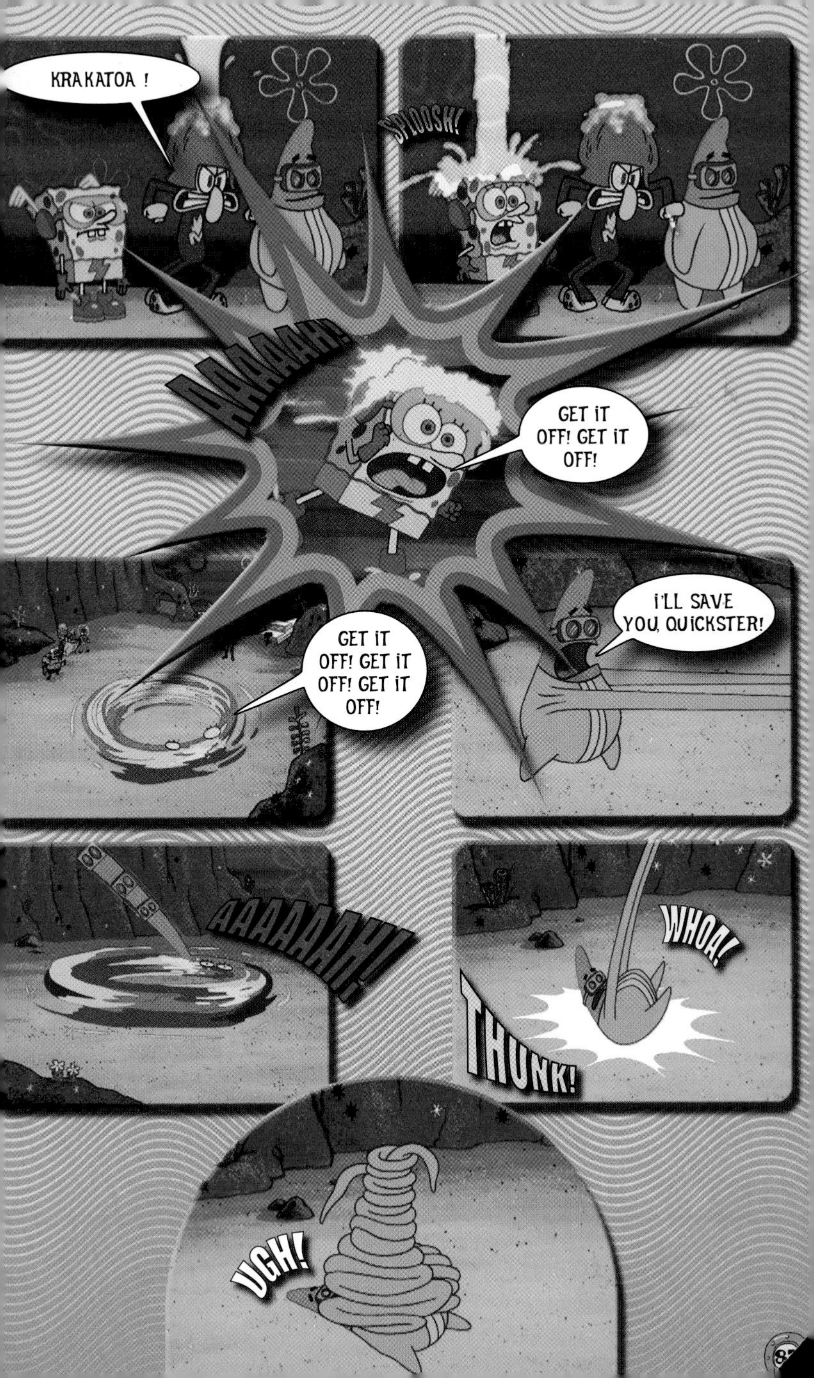
KRAKATOA !
SPLOOSH!
AAAAAH!
GET IT OFF! GET IT OFF!
I'LL SAVE YOU, QUICKSTER!
GET IT OFF! GET IT OFF! GET IT OFF!
AAAAAAH!!
WHOA!
THUNK!
UGH!

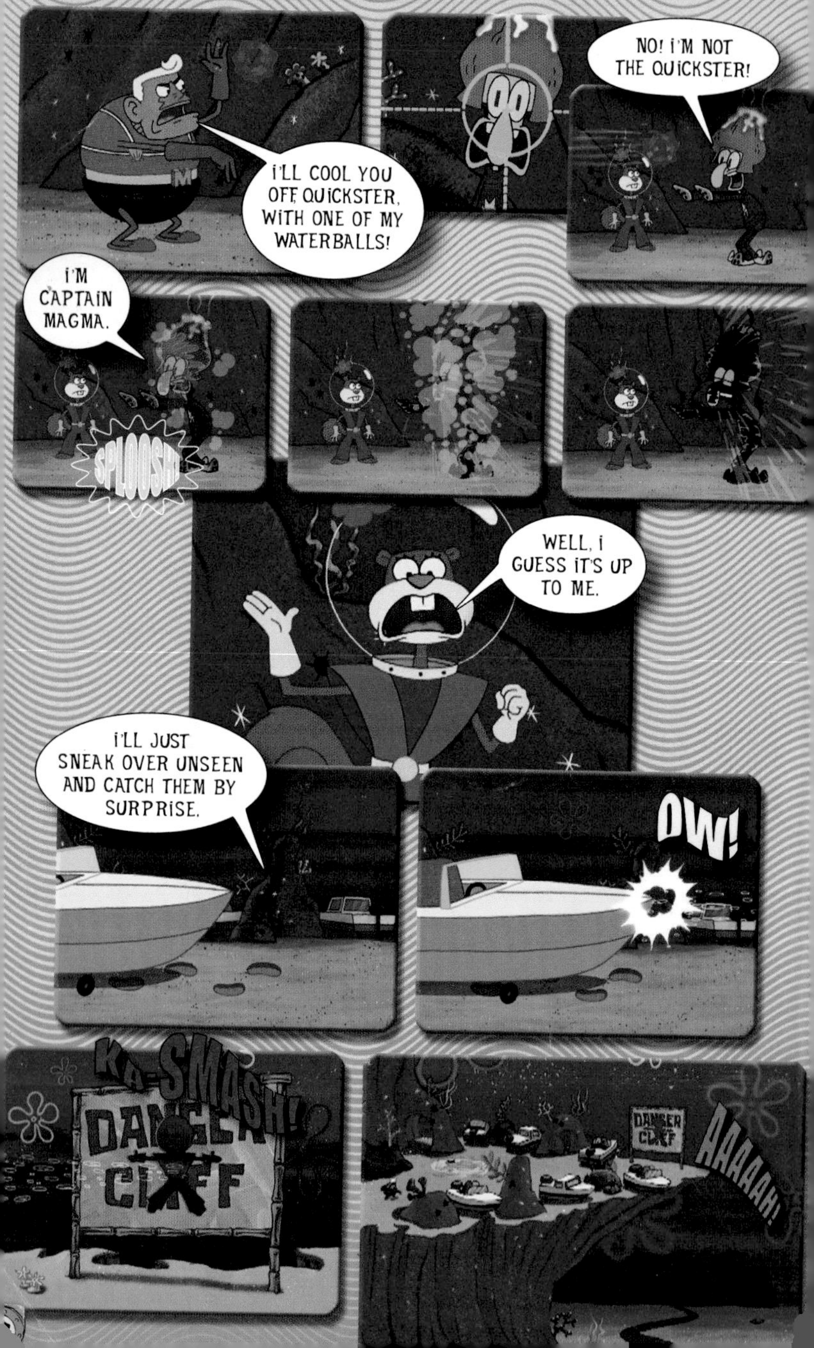

I'LL COOL YOU OFF, QUICKSTER, WITH ONE OF MY WATERBALLS!
NO! I'M NOT THE QUICKSTER!
I'M CAPTAIN MAGMA.
SPLOOSH!
WELL, I GUESS IT'S UP TO ME.
I'LL JUST SNEAK OVER UNSEEN AND CATCH THEM BY SURPRISE.
OW!
KA-SMASH!
DANGER CLIFF
DANGER CLIFF
AAAAAH!

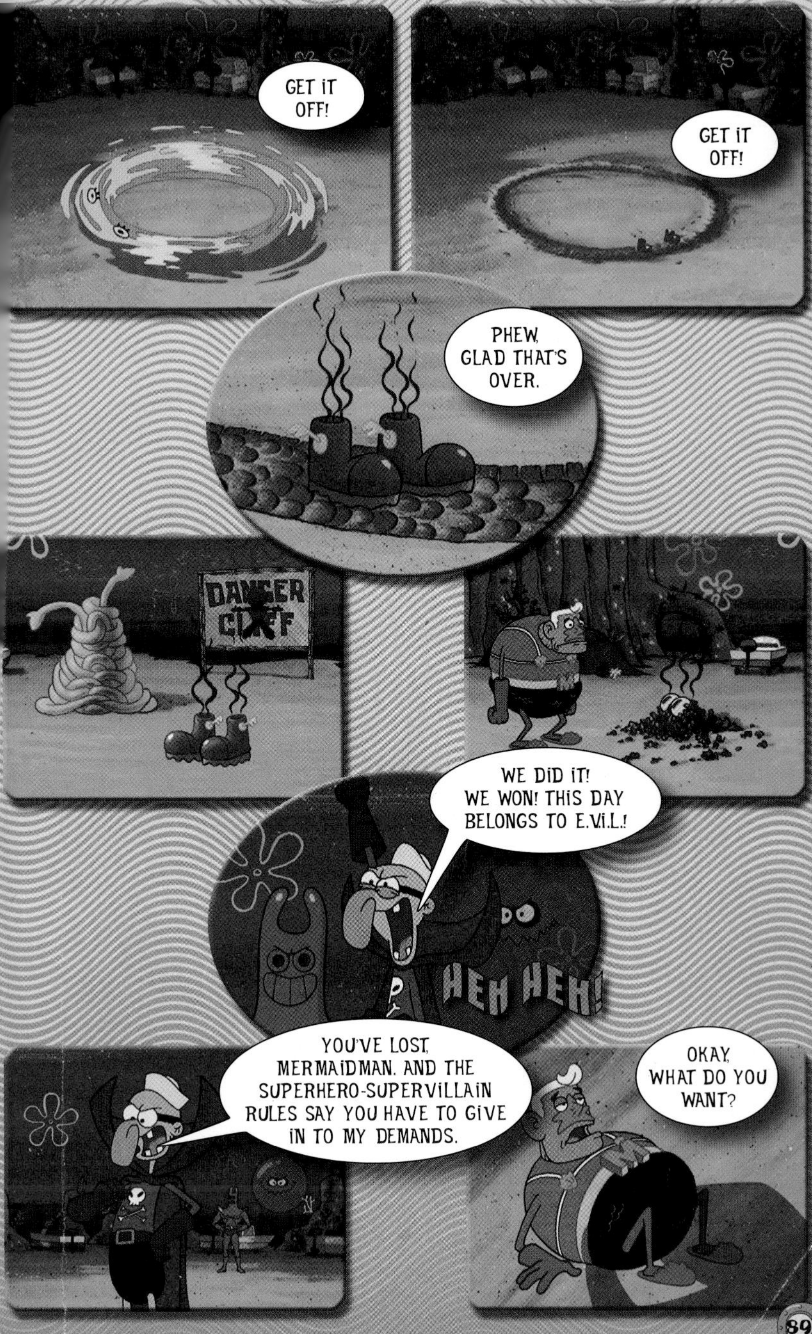
GET IT OFF!
GET IT OFF!
PHEW, GLAD THAT'S OVER.
DANGER CLIFF
WE DID IT! WE WON! THIS DAY BELONGS TO E.V.I.L.!
HEH HEH!
YOU'VE LOST, MERMAIDMAN. AND THE SUPERHERO-SUPERVILLAIN RULES SAY YOU HAVE TO GIVE IN TO MY DEMANDS.
OKAY, WHAT DO YOU WANT?

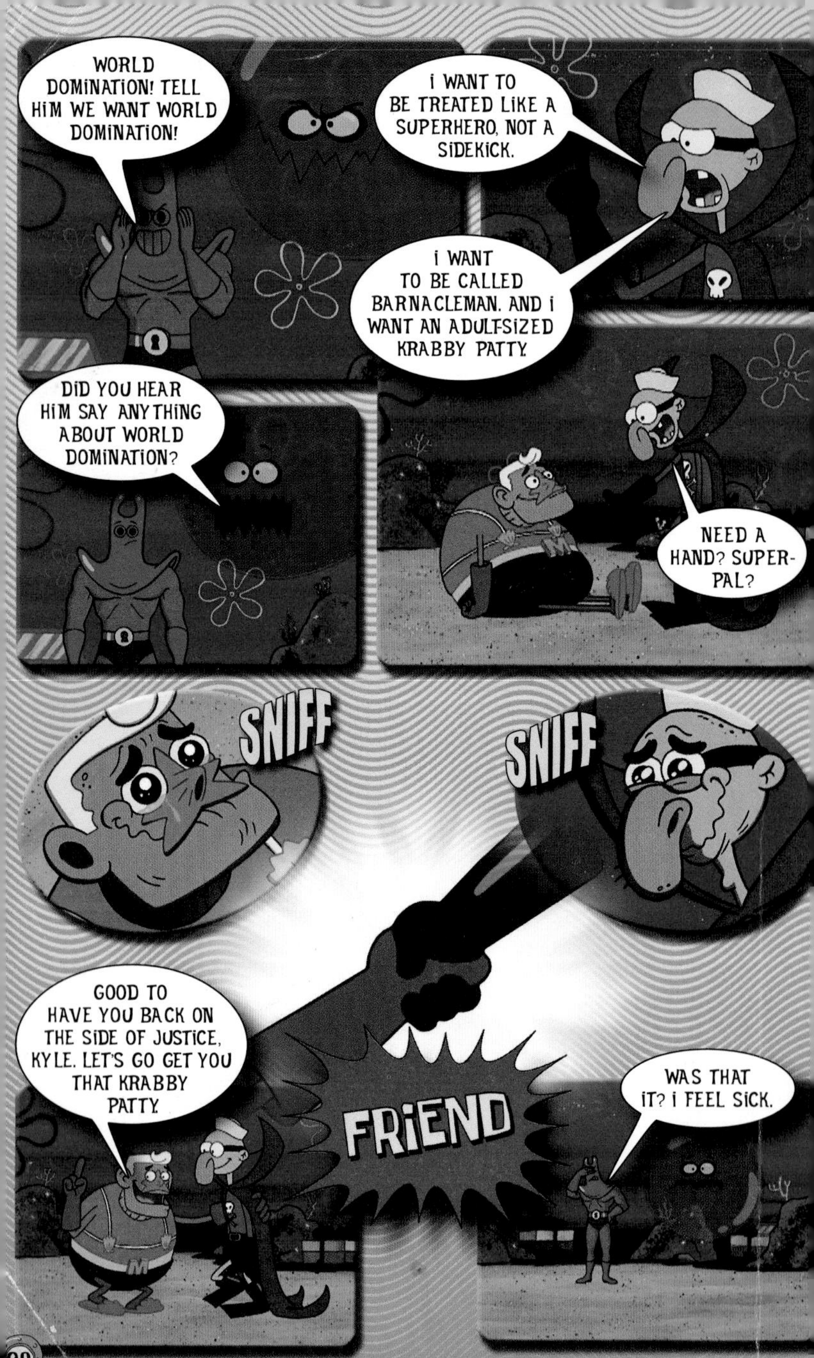
WORLD DOMINATION! TELL HIM WE WANT WORLD DOMINATION!
I WANT TO BE TREATED LIKE A SUPERHERO, NOT A SIDEKICK.
I WANT TO BE CALLED BARNACLEMAN. AND I WANT AN ADULT-SIZED KRABBY PATTY.
DID YOU HEAR HIM SAY ANYTHING ABOUT WORLD DOMINATION?
NEED A HAND? SUPER-PAL?
SNIFF
SNIFF
FRIEND
GOOD TO HAVE YOU BACK ON THE SIDE OF JUSTICE, KYLE. LET'S GO GET YOU THAT KRABBY PATTY.
WAS THAT IT? I FEEL SICK.

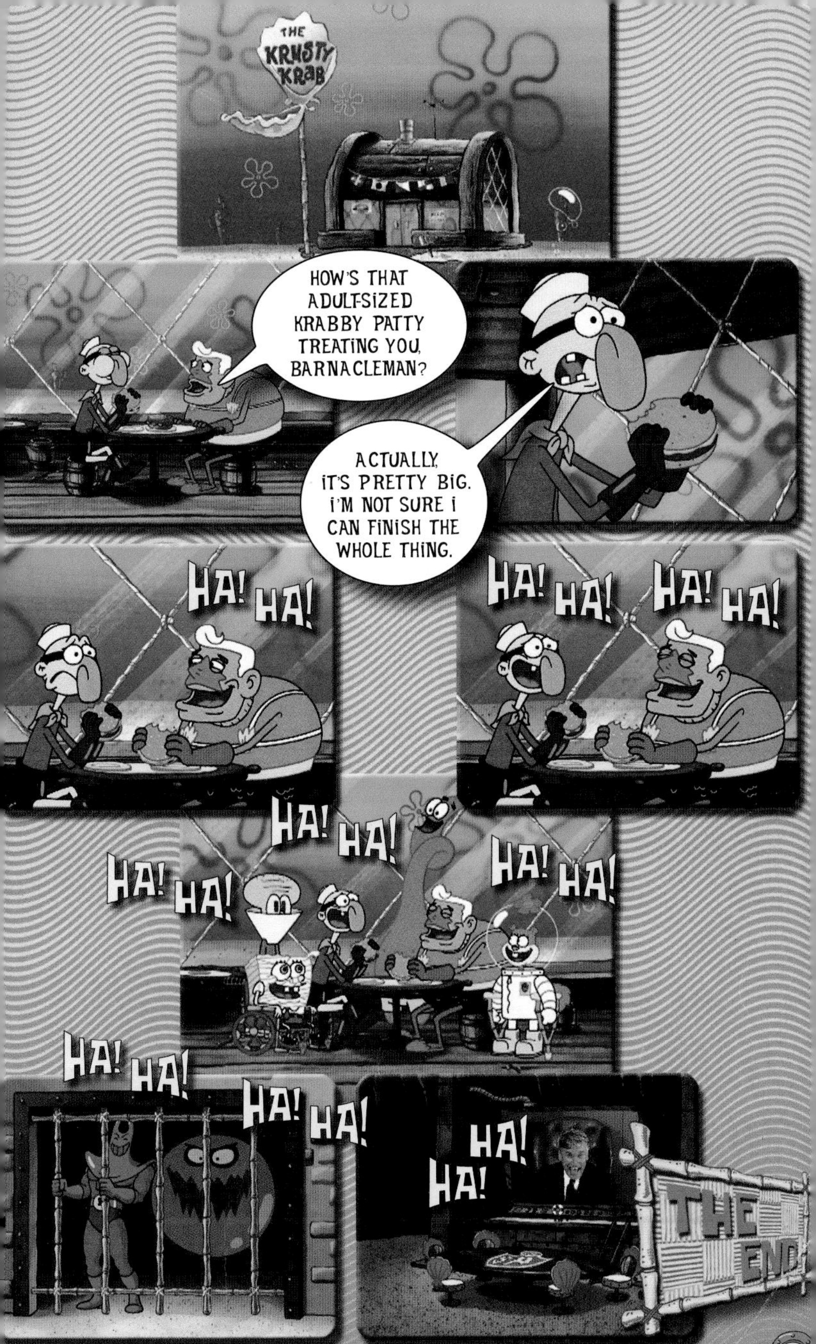
THE KRUSTY KRAB
HOW'S THAT ADULT-SIZED KRABBY PATTY TREATING YOU, BARNACLEMAN?
ACTUALLY, IT'S PRETTY BIG. I'M NOT SURE I CAN FINISH THE WHOLE THING.
HA! HA!
HA! HA! HA! HA!
HA! HA!
HA! HA!
HA! HA!
HA! HA!
HA! HA!
HA! HA!
THE END

Also available from TOKYOPO

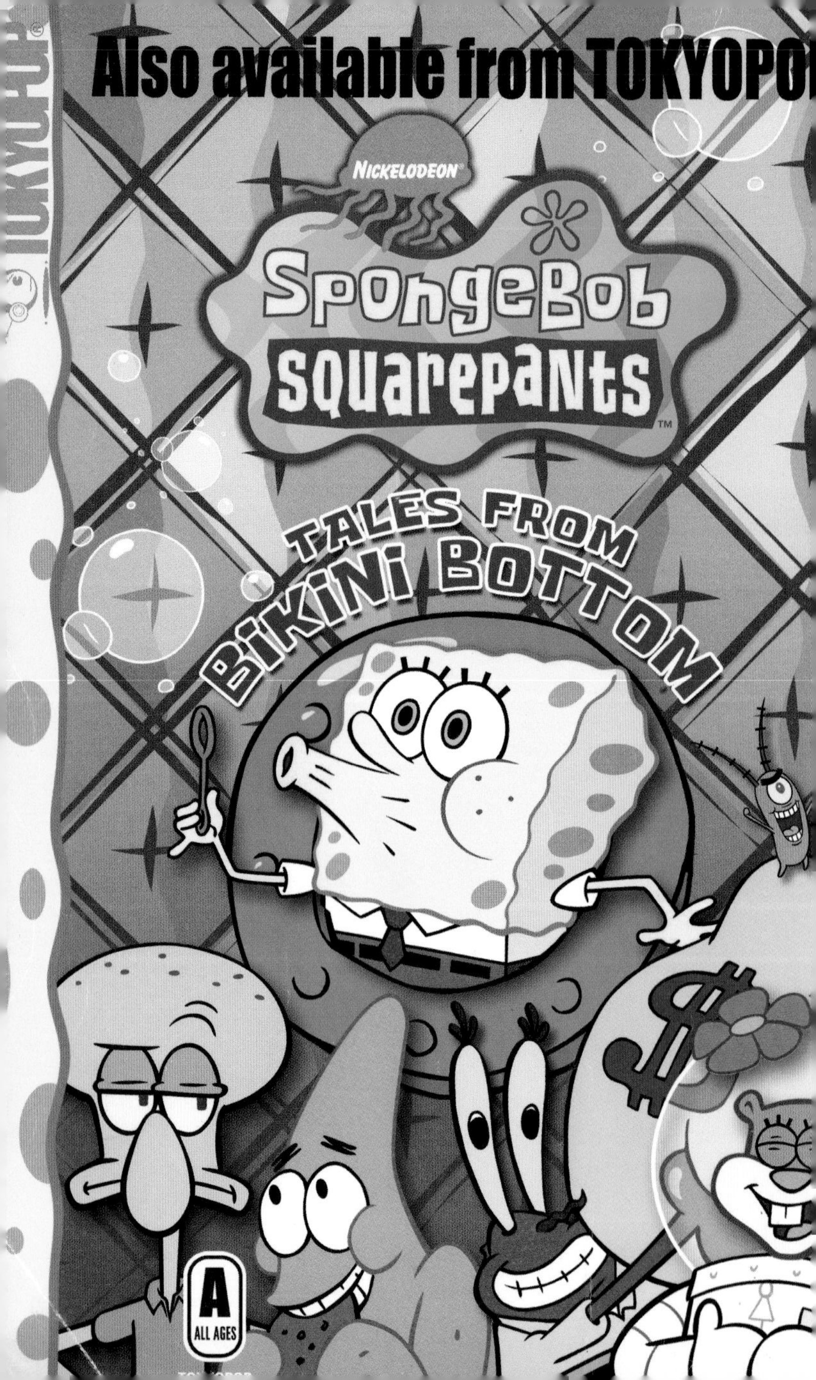
TOKYOPOP
NICKELODEON
SpongeBob SquarePants
TALES FROM BIKINI BOTTOM
A
ALL AGES